THE LIFE AND TIMES OF A SINGLE WOMAN

By

Colleen Riley Roberts

authorHOUSE™

1663 LIBERTY DRIVE, SUITE 200
BLOOMINGTON, INDIANA 47403
(800) 839-8640
WWW.AUTHORHOUSE.COM

First published by AuthorHouse 11/24/04

ISBN: 1-4184-9385-6 (e)
ISBN: 1-4184-9384-8 (sc)

Library of Congress Control Number: 2004096498

Printed in the United States of America
Bloomington, Indiana

This book is printed on acid-free paper.

Cover Photograph - The Author in 1978

Photography - Anthony Micallef

Dress by Marilyn Brooks

Occasion - annual picnic hosted by

Marilyn Brooks and Theo Dimson

At Theo's country estate

CREDITS

For my beloveds	My son, Robert Riley My late mother, Eleanor Riley
My Inner Belief Director	Saul I. Marks, M.D., F.R.C.P.(C) Psychiatrist
Books of Influence	*The Artist's Way* by Julia Cameron Sol Stein *On Writing* Stephen King - *A Memoir of the Craft - On Writing*
Friends & Family	Pulver Azman, Yank Azman, Marilyn Brooks, Dora Carrasco, Kennedy Coles, Patrick Conlon, Ellen Kerrivan, Evelyn Martin, Judy Robello, Armand Soucie, Rose-May Soucie Laderoute, Olivia Ruth
Special Kindness	Vivian Baker, Barbara Riley
Anonymous, Canadian Editor	He wrote, (Colleen Roberts) "writes with obvious personal charm." Those words sang to my soul when I needed help the most.
Editors	Kathleen Masurak, Emily Moriak
Spirits from a Higher Plane	Bernadette and Heather nudged me forward daily
Website	www.colleenrileyroberts.com

TABLE OF CONTENTS

INTRODUCTION

On a cold, winter night a few years ago, I was driving home after visiting my son Robert, taking my usual route on Dundas Street East. Cautious driving was called for on the icy roads. As I crossed the small bridge over the Don River, and reached the apex, I saw a man on a bicycle slide and fall to the ground dead center in the middle of the road about one hundred feet in front of me. My car kept moving forward but he lay stationary. My heart began to pound as I gingerly applied the brakes. I was worried he wouldn't get up, and worried too that I could hit an icy patch, lose control and slide right into him. It was terrifying for those few seconds, but he did get up and walked his bike to the sidewalk.

Driving down the apex, as I slowly began to move forward, a car pulled up behind me. Right up. The headlights flooded my space. The driver was impatient at my slow speed. All that was evident to him was a man walking a bike on the sidewalk. He was ticked off and drove just inches behind me. As we approached a red light on the other side of the bridge, he pulled up on my passenger side, rolled down the window and began screaming at me.

"You fucking bitch!" he yelled.

Our cars stopped at the intersection. His eyes fixed on me. He started shaking his fist at me and made a move to get out of his car. He looked at my locked passenger door. His eyes assessed the long walk around to the driver's side. He retreated, deciding instead to continue yelling profanities of the worst nature and particular to a woman's parts.

I burst out laughing. The light turned green and he sped off. As the hysteria diminished, I probed for insight on how my decisions, innocent or determined, affect others.

Many people stopped for me when I slipped. Many shared my triumphs, my joys and my insanities. I dedicate this book to them. And also, to my patient son Robert, who listened to every cornball idea of how I was going to be 'rich, rich, rich', and witnessed my broken heart over the man with whom I had a love affair.

The most important thread in my single life may or may not be the lifetime affair I had with a married rock star, but it is the most fascinating. He lived in the United States, and I lived in Canada. After meeting on a blind date, he took me to New York City for our first date. From then on, we wove into each other's lives with a mystery and excitement that kept me tantalized for thirty years.

This book is about the events that made up my life. Never into the nine-to-five idea of life, never having grasped that because I was a woman I wasn't born liberated, I have spent the last sixty-some years taking one step at a time. As each day arrived, I embraced it with a curiosity that has enriched my life since I was a child.

I still enjoy that curiosity.

CHAPTER ONE
MY EARLIEST YEARS

Had I not been born during WWII, when my birth was mingled not only with family tragedy but also with a grieving society facing the horrors of war, I may have avoided a time filled with darkness and tears that marked me for life. My fair skin and blonde hair was partly to blame.

On August 29, 1940, I was born in Ottawa, Ontario, Canada to a French-Canadian mother, Eleanor Laura Soucie, and a third generation Irish-Canadian father, George Cyril Riley. I never met my father. He died three months before I was born. My petite 4' 11" mother had been in mourning since May 9th, and all she ate was buttered popcorn. Hence, I bounced out at nine pounds and one ounce, filled with the fat cells I still own today. My father's seemingly innocent dying words were his wish that my mother would have a fair-haired daughter. This proved to be prophetic as these words became an agonizing litany for me. For years, my relations were moved to tears by my presence. Hate, too, was to enter this mournful world, but it was some time before I learned the reason why.

On May 9, 1940, my father died of appendicitis. It was at a time when doctors made house calls. My father lay in agony from early morning until that evening when the doctor finally arrived. He died in a hospital soon after.

My grandmother was grief stricken about losing her 22-year-old son. She would never resolve that grief and would eventually blame me for her son's death. She chose me to blame and would vent her hostility until the day she died.

Mom was left with a small insurance policy, me, and my one and a half-year-old brother, Rodney. Shortly thereafter we were put on Mother's Allowance, the old term for what is now known as welfare.

For a time, we stayed in my paternal grandparents' large Victorian home on Laurier Avenue West where a perennial garden with holly hocks and a huge weeping willow provided a natural amphitheater. There, with great joy, I hauled out the folding chairs and invited the neighborhood kids to see my show. The free ginger ale was a bigger inducement than my singing, but I was proud to stage, conduct, and promote the entire event on my own.

My life changed dramatically when my hero, Grandfather Dominique, passed away. I was five years old, and I kept touching his face as he lay in his satin lined casket amidst the Victorian furnishings in the front parlor. I waited for his loving smile to look back at me until my mother pulled me from his side. It was after the funeral that my grandmother, a thin, bent over, scraggily gray-haired woman in her early 70's intensified her hatred toward me. She ignored me while praising and doting on my brother. She avoided me, and when we did have eye contact, she looked at me with vehemence. I didn't know why.

We moved out of grandmother's house to a storefront home modified into an apartment on Percy Street in downtown Ottawa. The big store window in front was draped closed. For a kid it was fun. The front room was decorated with a big, cushy, maroon and green sofa set - donated of course. The war was over and poverty was everywhere, but there was also kindness. Being in the apartment meant that I was out from under the cruel scrutiny of my grandmother.

"Colleen. Colleen. Wake up!" mom called as I slept curled up in the big green chair, the same one I sat in on Christmas Eve waiting joyously for Santa with a plate full of cookies.

"It's time to get ready for the photographer," she called. I stirred awake, my hair wound in white rag strips from old sheets.

"I talked to Daddy," I told Mom.

She smiled. "You mean you dreamt of Daddy."

"No, Mummy. I talked to him. I talk to him every day. He's my friend."

My mother looked at me seriously and asked, "What do you talk about?"

"Daddy takes me to the store and buys me candy. And we go to the park and play." My face filled with joy. "He tells me stories."

Mom smiled. "Your Daddy's in heaven, and he loves you and watches over you. Now let's get you dressed and ready." Mom took out the rags, and my soft blonde hair twirled into ringlets.

She dressed me in a magnificent three piece, white knitted dress ensemble complete with tam, a hand-me-down from my cousin Marion. I was feeling so clean and pretty.

"Now go outside and tell your brother to come in so I can get him ready," my mother instructed.

I opened the front door and called out, "Rodney. You have to come in now and get dressed for the photographer."

Rodney and his friend Wayne Van Exan were busy making pies with the mud they found in the driveway. They looked up at me all dressed in white, held a brief consultation and the mud pies flew. Within seconds I was splattered all over: my ringlets, my face, and my three piece outfit. I went screaming into the house.

An hour later we were at the photographer's studio where I sat with straight limp hair, a blue gingham dress, and a face that refused to smile. I had to look at that tinted 8x10 photograph every time I visited my grandmother.

Not long after, Rodney took me to a gully and left me there. I stood alone, screaming. The gully was eight feet down in a dense forest patch. Barely a trickle of sunlight found its way in amongst the trees and bushes, and I began crying harder than I ever had. I spun around in desperation only to see trees and bushes filling my horizon. Finally, a stranger found me and brought me home. My brother, filled with the joy of play with his buddies, simply forgot about me. He would again in the future. Usually, he would leave me near a movie theater we had attended. I would knock on house doors until some kind person would take me in and call my mother. They often gave me milk and cookies until mom arrived.

The first Christmas gathering after my grandfather's death was held in my Aunt Judith's home with her husband and their two children. They lived in a small, three bedroom house on Sweetland Avenue. It was located on a hill a few doors up from the home of skating star Barbara Ann Scott. My small family of three had just moved in with them.

Aunt Judith had a frail figure like my grandmother (grandmonster) and used pursed lips to speak. It was part of the nouveau riche attitude of which no member of my family was a part, yet Aunt Judith tried desperately to adopt.

My mother, my brother, and I shared a bedroom, and my mother looked after the house and all the kids while my aunt took a part time job. Auntie insisted on meals precisely spooned out on large plates and no second helpings. However, from her own money and food stash, my mother prepared evening snacks for us. It was usually peanut butter and jam sandwiches, and she hid them in our dresser. There, hushed in darkness, we would munch behind stifled giggles.

Auntie was never happy about anything and easily moved to disgust, as she was when I thought I could fly. One morning, I awoke believing several angels guided me everywhere and that I could fly with them. That morning, I stepped on the front veranda, climbed onto the railing, spread my arms and attempted flight. Instead, I crashed onto the grass and my wrist broke in three places. Getting me to the hospital meant everyone would be late for work. Auntie was flapping up and down the hall with her pursed lips cursing my stupidity.

It was Christmas 1946 when my grandmother began to taunt me. The household and my grandmother gathered around a huge decorated tree to open our gifts before going to my Great Aunt Margaret's for a traditional dinner. We were excited. Uncle Harry was the official gift distributor.

He handed Rodney two presents from Grandma. One contained a gold ring, and the other was a ticket to go to Detroit, Michigan with grandma and visit family. Grandmother smiled as everyone let out an "ah".

Uncle Harry picked up a scruffy envelope with the name "Colleen" scrawled on it. He looked over at my grandmother and whispered, "Is this from you?" Grandmother nodded a defiant yes, her eyes avoiding me.

"And here we have a present for Colleen from Grandma," he said.

There was disgust in my little eyes as I accepted the dirty envelope, slowly opened it, and found two quarters inside. I wanted to cry as nobody said anything about how mean and awful my gift was. There was a stunned silence. No one spoke. Not a word. I don't remember, but I think I said thank you. I must have because it was then that I began the pitiful journey of needing grandma's love.

My own mother had been orphaned early, having lost her mother when she was five and her father when she was twelve. But I didn't need my grandmother's love because she was my only grandparent left. It was because I felt her hate and that was unacceptable.

Later, at Great Aunt Margaret's Christmas dinner party, Grandma launched a verbal attack on me. We were in the kitchen when she began her assault.

"It's her fault my son is dead," she said as she pointed to me. "She had to come into the world and for that God took my son away. I hate her. Don't let her near me."

Great Aunt Margaret rescued me, taking me to sit beside my mother around a lavishly decorated Victorian table set for twelve where various family members were seated. I snuggled close to my mom, sheepishly looking around. I believed the whole family knew about the guilt of my birth and how much my grandmother hated me. But I didn't understand why my aunt or anyone else didn't try to make things better. Grandma gave me mean looks and even growled at me a few times but nobody said anything. The turkey was served, the wine flowed, and all were festive while I wondered why no one cared about me. How could they be so mean?

Finally, my Great Aunt Margaret hugged me and told me, "I will act as your grandmother from now on."

For a long time she was really wonderful, but it came at the cost of letting my grandmother terrorize me. I was both ostracized and accepted as my aunts, uncles, and mother sat tight-lipped. This crazed woman now had carte blanche to treat me however she wanted, while doting on my brother.

The fifty-cent gift became the norm and at times she refused to sit at the same dinner table with me. Up she would get from the glorious dining table at family occasions. Off she would go in dramatic tears (I do believe the wine helped), crying at the loss of her son, my father, while I, the guilty party, sat at the dining room table shaking and hugging my mother. Her unruly, scraggly gray hair, wrinkled skin, edgy demeanor, and dominant voice should have terrified me, but instead I longed for acceptance. I had lost my father and my grandfather. But grandmother was alive, so maybe there was hope for her love.

That Christmas night I was consumed with guilt. Was my father's death my fault? I cried the night away, totally confused about life and death. At six years old I felt very much alone. I could not face my imaginary father ever again. Family members had told me a child born under my circumstances would always have a sad face. Little did they know how deep and twisted that sadness would become. They compared my look to the stoic face of Joan of Arc when the movie starring Ingrid Bergman was released. Although my enthusiastic temperament forced me out of a recurring depression and pushed me into achievement, I felt obligated to show the world the sad face that accompanied my birthright.

Not long after Christmas, we moved into the vacant Russian Embassy on Chapel Street that was abandoned during the war. Our mover, a family friend named John, volunteered to move us for free. He was a burly man in his fifties with a Ukrainian accent. He was in the junk and scrap business and rode around town in a huge, splintered, open flatbed pulled by a horse.

All loaded up, our belongings were centered in the wide flatbed, covered with blankets, and mom and Rodney and I huddled against the pile looking down the street. We were a sight to behold. The neighbors watched and snickered as the flatbed made its way, moving us to our home a few streets over on the top side of the hill.

Mom felt my uneasiness. "Hold your head up, Colleen. Be proud of who you are." But I was mortified. Relief began to flow through me as we turned the corner toward our new home away from our neighbor's peering eyes.

A man named Boris had assumed uninvited residence in the vacated Russian Embassy. He, in turn, invited poor families to join him in the three-story habitat. For this, we counted our blessings. The only financial obligation was $15.00 a month to cover light and heat, and without an actual hand out, we took a chance on how long we could live there.

Rodney was nine years old and I was eight, and both of us felt a sense of adventure living in the Embassy. Because we were fatherless, we received special attention. We were given a grand third-floor corner room with its own three piece ensuite with the largest bathtub I had ever seen. Other "homes" were in offices, and tenants shared stall washrooms. Mom quickly made us a comfortable home, dividing the space with curtains stretched across wires. We all slept in a cozy, chenille-covered double bed. Our dresser top served as a kitchen counter, and mom organized a hot plate. The mystique of Russia fascinated us, and we were soon running through the building looking for secret rooms and listening devices. We believed our suite was the headquarters for a Russian spy.

The local newspapers got hold of the story and headlined it "Squatter's Rights." Mom was shattered with the circumstances of her life: widowed at age twenty-two with two children, surrounded by poverty, and now the story of our make shift home all over the newspaper. More than ever she was determined to get off welfare.

Located a half block from Laurier Avenue, the strip known as "Embassy Row", I considered our new home a major step up. The quality of our neighbors in fine houses was inspiring, and the grand residence of former Prime Minister Mackenzie King was at the corner. Every Halloween we were invited to knock at the door, where we were treated with an abundance of apples and candy. I used to shiver with excitement.

It was there, living in poverty but witnessing wealth, that my dreams of getting out began to develop. The transformation from my identity as a child of welfare into the fantasy of living like the rich came about a year after we moved in.

In 1951, Princess Elizabeth (later Queen) and her husband the Duke of Edinburgh made a visit to Canada, and the Duke actually touched my hand amongst hundreds of others as I stood in my Brownie uniform in front of a hotel in downtown Ottawa. It was a proud moment, but more eventful was the discovery of the most enchanting hotel I had ever visited, the Chateau Laurier. Floating with the grace of the Duke's majestic touch, I entered the hotel in search of a washroom. I was awestruck and wandered through the hotel for hours. There I discovered architecture, history, art deco interiors of incredible proportions, political history, and the swimming pool. After an inquiry, I learned that I could swim at the pool and lie on the deck chairs like the rich people for only fifty cents.

And that's what I did. I became the best errand girl around and used the money earned to spend Saturdays at the pool. Comfy chaise lounges were each stacked with an abundance of towels, surrounding the pool. Off in my dream world, I would swim and then walk like a princess to my chair with my head tilted and eyes searching for acceptance. It didn't matter whether other guests were there. I was into my trip. Even now, when I visit my family in Ottawa, I still go to the Chateau Laurier for breakfast, and I enjoy a dinner or two on the terrace overlooking the locks and the Ottawa River. Zoe's dining room is my all-time favorite spot for a holiday buffet.

In the early times, my Great Aunt Margaret had furnished me with small bits of family jewelry. A little bee pin on my jacket made me socially acceptable for special outings. However, the Russian Embassy was a complex of assorted families. There were little "Fagans" about, and it wasn't long before the lot was stolen along with our milk money. Those demons also taught me to shop without money. They took me to a downtown department store, egging me on until I finally pocketed a balloon and a small rubber ball. Leaving the store, I was in terror. The emotion grew as I made my way home and the fantasy of police taking me away engulfed me. Once home, I took out a spoon and dug a hole in the front lawn, ripped the balloon to shreds, and buried it with the ball. For weeks I kept surveillance on the dig spot. The police never did arrive.

The Russian Embassy was reclaimed in 1950, and we moved to a nice flat across from Osgoode Street Public School which I had attended since grade one. Comprised of two rooms on the third floor, our new flat did not have running water. We had chores like hauling up jugs of water, hauling down the dirty dishwater, and climbing three flights down and up with the laundry. But we had two spacious rooms and eventually took a third room on the second floor for Rodney. Mom used to make a meal she referred to as the King's Dinner. It was chopped wieners, macaroni, onions and tomatoes over toast. Unless we were invited out, this special dish would constitute our Thanksgiving meal served on a fresh oilcloth table square. We were a tight team, the three of us, and our theme song for these special, at home dinners was, "The Navy get the gravy, the Army get the beans, and the Riley's get the leftovers."

Mom started working as a waitress in a big, upscale department store on Sparks Street named Murphy Gambles. Although her income did little to improve our impoverished life, she was embarrassed by charity. A real sense of pride filled our home now that everything came from her earnings. Eventually mom advanced to sales in children's wear, and I was soon wearing quality finery. I could only have one or two outfits a year, but they were the best. I loved fabric and sewing, and my dolls usually won "Best Dressed" doll contests. I now had access to the finest fabrics and sought deals in the remnants bin. In the yard goods department, I also discovered the fabric of the day: floral chintz. Our home took on a magazine look after I covered orange crates, trunks, and lampshades with coordinating colors of the fabric.

Despite our poverty, mom always looked beautiful. Her upswept hair was always coifed. Mostly, she wore a "rat" (a soft brown cotton roll wrapped in a net) pinned under her hair for a pompadour look. Not only was it fashionable in wartime, but at only 4' 11", both high heels and high hair gave her stature. Similar to her sister Lovina and her niece Nelda, she loved fashionable clothing and dressed with gusto - a trait of French-Canadian women. Whenever they were together there was always a collection of cosmetics, powder, and lipstick. Perfume permeated the air. I reveled in it.

By the time I reached grade six, my organizing skills were evident and they translated to a lot of power for a ten-year-old. The students did the school patrolling, and I was captain of the Safety Patrols - the first woman on the job. Being in the principal's class that year, I was also secretary to the secretary. In the event she was out, I answered the phone in the adjacent office. In addition, I was the school bell ringer, the choir conductor for the twice-weekly assembly, and even starred in the school play. I played "Topsy," a young black girl in *Uncle Tom's Cabin*. It took three weeks and many disgruntled scrubbings by the landlady to rid the bathtub of all the black shoe polish.

I was always active in pursuing my interests. When I found out there was an evening tap dancing class in my school, I attended the class once a week. I couldn't afford the fees, so I watched through the hallway window and then ran home to practice in the basement on the hard cement floor. As the end of the season drew near, the kind teacher asked me to show her what I had learned. She liked what I did, and put me in the final recital, inviting my mother to attend.

We were Catholics and attended St. Joseph's Church on Laurier Avenue every Sunday. I didn't like church and eventually left my mother sitting in the main floor pews while I ran for a front row balcony seat. From that vantage point, I could count all the red hats. My mother was not pleased when I gave her the weekly count.

I took the Catholic sacrament of confirmation when I was ten years old. I prepared by professing my first confession, a deed to clear my soul of all sins. If one had a mortal sin on their soul, they could not receive communion. With three mortal sins, one could not go to heaven. The priest had the power to absolve the sins by granting forgiveness and assigning appropriate penance according to the sin.

As I knelt in the confessional, the priest heard about the theft of the balloon and ball, but then I drew a blank. I could not think of any other sins. The priest asked if I had ever yelled at my mother.

"No," I answered. "I can't recall yelling at my mom."

"Well," the priest said. "Do you ever get angry at your mother inside and not express it?"

I had to respond, "Yes."

"Well," he told me. "It's a sin to feel anger toward your mother."

I felt anger inside a lot of times and hence spent many hours examining the paintings of the twelve Stations of the Cross. Vulnerable to having the finger of guilt pointed at me, these words served as another bed of confusion and insecurity. If feeling anger was a sin, I sensed that expressing it would be intolerable. So began my inability to say what I felt unless it was good news. Perhaps, my lifetime fear had seeded itself. But maybe it could have been worse if I had confessed the weekly counting of the red hats.

My life was consumed with the pursuit of glamour. The lure of figure skating was the strongest, particularly since Barbara Ann Scott had perfected figure eights on my community rink. However, no matter how many eights I attempted, I did not have the skills. Later I tried roller skating at the new Minto Indoor Rink. Gliding on the floor on wheels gave me a wonderful feeling. I learned how to waltz and participated in shows, including a special show in Montreal, Quebec. My hope was to become a professional until my accident. My front wheel locked with my partner's wheel, and I went flying over backward and was knocked out on the floor. It was discomforting to awake to an entire audience gasping while I lay motionless. I wanted their applause not their pity. A stretcher carried me away with the crowds wishing me well. Once back on my feet, I gave up performing in shows.

The stress-buster of the day was white margarine, the new budget priced spread aiming to take the place of butter. It came in a clear plastic bag with a small, indented button in the center of the bag filled with coloring. To get the margarine to look like yellow butter, you would bust the button by squeezing it and then continue to squeeze the bag until the color was blended throughout. This took about half an hour. The task was usually relegated to the kids. I would sit in the living room squeezing the bag while watching Rodney pound his fists into the back of the sofa every time "Boston Blackie" punched a crook on his radio show. On Sunday night, I squeezed away while curled up listening to "Lux Presents

Hollywood." I hated the taste of margarine and refused to eat it. On mom's budget, she and Rodney stayed with margarine while the icebox also contained a pound of butter for me.

One thing Rodney and I agreed on was having a hobby. Rodney was into building and flying model airplanes. He hung each plane in strategic flying formation over his bed, saluting and saying "good night and good flying," every bedtime. My hobby was dolls, and I had a collection of eight including the freckled-faced "Maggie Muggins," star of a radio show of the same name. The show always ended with Maggie saying, "I wonder what will happen tomorrow, Mr. McGarrity." I would recant those words to Maggie every night while anticipating what the following day would bring for each of us. Every doll was smartly dressed in fashions I sewed up, including dresses with matching hats, underpinnings, and a couple of fur coats made up from mom's old Persian lamb coat. At night I would get them into their nightgowns, place them on the floor, cover them up, and say goodnight.

On summer evenings in Ottawa one could hear the nightly gunshots of police exterminating pigeons. It was their responsibility to reduce their numbers. Pellet guns in hand, they would raise their arms high and shoot those poor creatures sitting on the ledges of some magnificent architecture building, picking them off one at a time. I identified with these pigeons; I felt vulnerable. With tears of confusion falling down my face, I prayed for the souls of the innocent pigeons, and asked God to help grandma love me.

CHAPTER TWO
GREAT AUNT MARGARET

Great Aunt Margaret was an imposing figure of grand proportions who radiated warmth to everyone around her. A tall woman, she weighed around 250 lbs. and wore floral patterned housedresses. Most of the time, she was covered with an apron. Feeding me was one of her favorite good deeds. On one early visit when I was about eight months old, still on the bottle, and crying my heart out, she looked at my mother and declared, "That child is hungry." Off she ran to the kitchen to prepare mashed carrots and potatoes covered in butter. From then on, she spoiled me with food on every visit. Family members would always say that I would grow up to look just like my Great Aunt Margaret. Despite my efforts to prove them wrong . . . well, let's not jump ahead. She loved the kitchen and was always preparing, canning, preserving or baking. In fact, she had two kitchens, and the most fun was the summer kitchen where the big corn feasts took place. There was always a big pot of corn simmering on the old wood stove - far more corn than we could eat. And only at Great Aunt Margaret's home were we pushed to slather on lots of butter.

Not insulated and therefore much cooler than the house, the summer kitchen had natural barn siding and a peaked roof. It was a large room housing a huge pine harvest table and seating for twelve.

It also served as a pantry and housed shelves of jams and preserves. The lighting was an old bulb hanging on a wire.

Margaret married late in life, around age 45, to a wonderful man named Jim Ullett. Although they never had children together, Jim had two older children from a previous marriage. When I was five years old, Great Aunt Margaret was sixty-five.

Her house was on the outskirts of Ottawa on the main artery of Richmond Road. It was set back from the street about 100 feet by a massive green lawn and wonderful huge trees. In what was more like a park setting, the large wood-framed house had a sweeping front veranda that wrapped around the house on one side. An old art deco metal swing sat on the side porch, and an old wooden swing in the side garden was always a lure for me when we visited. Great Aunt Margaret could watch us from the kitchen window and knew when a tray full of ginger ale would be welcome.

Corn stalks were abundant in the spacious back garden, running about a hundred feet deep, along with all the vegetables one could plant. Uncle Jim loved gardening and his plants provided lots of vegetables for preserving and canning. Rhubarb framed the outer fence and an apple tree stood as conductor in front of the garden.

The house was built sometime in the late 1800s and the interior was filled with art nouveau décor and a wonderful pair of large dark oak arts and crafts chairs. A bronze, figural lamp with robes flowing and a hand in the air, graced the mahogany staircase rail. Great Aunt Margaret took care in the appearance of her home, and every few years the functional furniture was sent out for refinishing. It was a dramatic contrast to my own home's humble furnishings, but I appreciated the splendor of each and every piece. I loved sleepovers when I would curl up in the finest white linens and sleep in a Victorian bed.

Visits with Great Aunt Margaret were exciting. Contained in her attic were the trappings she wore as a social butterfly in earlier times: plume fans, silver purses, flowing silk gowns, and hats of all shapes and sizes. For me, visiting the attic was not necessarily easy. Great Aunt Margaret would fill it with intrigue and the things that kids only ever saw in the movies.

"What are you going to do today, Colleen?" she asked on one of my visits. "I hope you're not thinking of going into that dirty old attic," she continued with a smile.

"Oh no, Aunt Margaret," I lied. "I'll just play around the house." My little heart was racing with excitement because the attic was exactly where I was headed as soon as her back was turned.

The second floor entrance to the attic was through a rickety, hinged door located three feet up from the floor and far too high to climb up without a foot stool. It was in the bathroom, and a step stool was always in front of the door when I was visiting alone.

I didn't think Great Aunt Margaret had a clue that I would make my way up to the attic. When the opportune moment came, I slipped up the stairs and cringed each time the floor creaked. For hours my heart was filled with the joy of fantasy as I played dress up and danced around the room in gowns of silk, wonderful hats, and always a plume fan in my hand. There were great trunks full of treasures, old rocking chairs, and mirrors, filling my day with dreams while sunlight trickled through the dormer window. Eventually I was played out and made my way back to the kitchen. There I stood with the look of innocence all over my soot-covered face.

"Hello, Colleen," Aunt Margaret said as she walked to the stove. "I just made some peanut butter cookies." Then she turned back, looked at me, and said, "You didn't play in the attic did you?"

"Oh no, Aunt Margaret," I lied again.

"That's good," she said. "Now wash up, and we'll have some cookies and milk."

Later I tinkered on her piano. I often brought music sheets, written by my father. I tried to bring his music to life. Self-taught, I could play traditional tunes like "God Save the King." Well, I thought I could play them. In any case, it was a spiritual connection to my father. I knew his fingers had touched the keyboard. I so hoped to feel his love.

Whether I was in the attic, munching away on freshly baked cookies or tinkering on the piano, Great Aunt Margaret's home was always an oasis of abundance. It was in her generous presence that I discovered mystery, mischievousness, fantasy and music, social graces, kindness, and much more. For that I am thankful. It came at a cost, however. Great Aunt Margaret's loyalty was with her sister, my grandmother, who continued to openly verbalize scathing attacks

22

on me. I wish I could have just felt humbled at grandma's insanity, but I also felt unloved. This feeling would never leave me.

CHAPTER THREE
MY FRENCH FAMILY

My mother's family, the Soucie family of Fort Coulounge, Quebec, had all the joy, laughter, and love I needed to establish a base of self-confidence. Mother was from a family of fourteen children with four sisters and nine brothers. One sister remained in Fort Coulounge and married, and the three others, including my mom, moved to Ottawa in search of husbands. All were successful and continued to live and raise families in Ottawa. Most of her brothers married and remained in Coulounge. Together, this family provided me with forty-five cousins.

The bus trip to Fort Coulounge was eighty miles northwest up the Ottawa River and was easy to make. Mother enjoyed visiting her family. I usually had a sick stomach on the way up which magically disappeared when I arrived. I had a reputation.

"Sit her at the front of the bus," the regular bus drivers would sternly direct my mother when they saw me coming, "so she can get out fast." They didn't view me as a cute kid.

I was closest to Uncle Joe, whom I called 'Daddy Joe', and his wife Aunt Diane. She used to rip a piece of paper from a brown paper bag and place it on my chest under my dress to prevent me from being sick on my return trip. Their children, my cousins Rose May, Annette, Yalonde, Roland, and Donald, loved to spoil me.

They made clothing for me, dressed me up, did my hair in ringlets, and paraded me out to the ice cream parlor in the center of town. Donald was handy with wood and made pine furniture for my dolls. One winter, he made a pine sled in which the family dog could pull me. But the dog always threw me off, and I'd tumble out, laughing, into the snow.

The small town of 2,000 made visiting family members easy. My cousin Armand, who later became Deputy Police Chief in Ottawa, operated a mink farm on his father's 250 acre estate just outside of town. The site contained two private lakes, one of which was easily accessible for my cousins and me. A rowboat on the shore was always ready for a voyage to the uninhabitable side of the lake. Awed by the mystique of the dense, uncharted forest, my cousin Darcy used to row my cousins and me to the other side, cautiously slowing the pace as we neared the shore. A cliff drop at water's edge prevented disembarking, and we were terrified that the boat might tip over. Darcy often gave the boat a little rock to hear us gasp, but mostly we sat still conjuring up images of creatures in the wild forest or of giant snakes circling the boat waiting for one of us to put our fingers in the water.

It was also at Armand's that I learned to ride horses. They were big, old, tired workhorses, and I had to ride bareback. But I enjoyed lumbering across the fields, using their manes to give directions. I learned to clean the stables and rub down my newfound friends. One day, when the sun was pouring out temperatures in the high eighties, I returned from riding and hosed down my horse. As I guided him to his stall, he looked at me as never before. His eyes said thank you. I was drawn to horses forever more.

One summer morning Armand invited me to feed the mink. Well, I had probably pushed him into that invitation. In a large field were rows and rows of mink cages and aisles wide enough to let a horse and dolly ride through. A tall barrel of ground meat sat on the dolly. The aroma soon stirred the mink, and they paced up and down their cages. Armand handed me a large splintered wooden spatula.

"Watch your fingers, Colleen," he said. "Those creatures will bite them off. Just spoon out the meat and slop it through the top of the cage where their food tray hangs."

Off we went, weaving our way through the cages with the flatbed dolly wavering from side to side over the bumpy path. The mink raced to their trays, and I could easily imagine my tiny hands being gobbled up in seconds. The chore completed, I thanked Armand and made no mention of wanting to do it again. I was more terrified than I was willing to admit.

Summer holidays in Fort Coulounge also included many visits to my Uncle Leo and Aunt Rosie's house. I especially liked to see my cousin Caroline. We had fun in the fields calling Bossie the cow at five in the morning for breakfast milking or out in the huge garden picking fresh vegetables for dinner. We also picked potatoes. Well, I let my cousins pick them while I sat on the living room floor filling a large bowl. The potatoes actually grew in the crawl space under the floor! Every day, a scatter carpet was removed to expose a trap door. One of Aunt Rosie's fifteen children, on potato rotation, would climb into the crawl space and toss out the fresh potatoes. The starchy vegetable would be peeled and cooked for the evening meal.

Best of all, however, was the simple calm at the end of the day. Caroline and I would sit on the front porch in the still of the night. Interspersed with girl talk, we would listen to the songs of the crickets and feast our eyes on the magic lights of the fireflies.

At other times, Daddy Joe took me pheasant hunting or his daughters took me berry picking. Although we would spend all afternoon climbing the hills where the berry patches were abundant, we never brought back full baskets. We intended to, but after using all that energy, we needed nourishment for the long walk home. With our stained lips, we would present Aunt Diane with our half-filled baskets. Since my aunt cooked fresh pies every day, we were given the chance to redeem ourselves regularly.

In this predominately French speaking town, wherever I went, someone in the family would always say, "Speak in English, Colleen is here." Here, I felt loved - in a town over which my grandmother had no influence.

The French are known for their French fries, and this did not escape me. With large families, the amount of potatoes consumed at dinner was grand, and peeling them was something a child could do. It was a chore most of my cousins wanted to avoid. But I thought peeling potatoes was fun and was thrilled to be in the assembly line in preparation for the evening meal. Within no time, I had worked myself up to summer peeler at a french fries stand. My Uncle Palma had opened the stand around 1947 in the center of town.

He had served in the military in Dieppe during the war and later returned to Fort Coulounge to run a cab stand from a small cabin next door to Labine's Hotel. He had dreams of opening a movie theater. Money was scarce, and the cab stand was not a booming business. He spent most days and evenings in the cabin with a radio and a hot plate. I loved to hear Uncle Palma tell the story of his french fries stand, especially with his French accent.

One Friday night some of the locals were inside Labine's having a few beers when one of them left to go home for dinner. En route he passed my Uncle Palma's cabstand and smelled the aroma of potatoes cooking.

"What's cooking, Palma?" he asked, rocking on his heels as he stood.

Palma shouted through the open window, "It's my dinner. I'm frying potatoes."

"Well, they smell good. I want your potatoes," the man said.

Palma was indignant. "You can't have them. It's my dinner."

The man sang out, "I'll give you one dollar for them."

"Hold on," Palma said. "You can have them."

Off went the bar patron back into the hotel with his dinner. His cronies looked up.

"Where'd you get the potatoes?" they questioned.

"Palma opened a french fries stand next door. He's selling them for one dollar."

Out went the group to order.

Palma asked them to return in ten minutes. He ran across the street to the general store and bought a ten-pound bag of potatoes for fifteen cents. A friend awaited him on his return.

"Hi, Palma," he said. "I hope you can help me out."

"What's the problem?" Palma asked as he began peeling the potatoes.

"I'm on my hotel route to drop off pop, but they pulled me off the road for too much tonnage. Would you let me store twelve cases of pop until Monday morning?"

"Sure," Palma said. "Just pile them in the corner."

As the truck pulled away, out staggered the customers. Noticing the pop boxes, one of them clambered, "I see you've got pop, too. I'll have a Coke."

The evolution of cabstand to French fry stand happened overnight. The townsfolk lined up for the fries, and the pop sold out by Monday morning. During my summer holidays, I sat on the grass behind Palma's stand, churning the cement potato peeler in exchange for all the fries I could eat. Five years later, Palma and my Uncle Hector opened the town's first movie theater with kitchen chairs for seating. Another five years later, they built a modern movie theater.

My summers in Coulounge were the best days I remember of my childhood. There, my large family owned, operated, or managed a great number of the businesses. They ran farms and looked after large families. Through it all, they still had time for me. In their power I felt shielded. In their embrace I felt respected. In my heart I felt loved.

CHAPTER FOUR
EARLY TEENS

At eleven years old, my life was becoming expensive. So I explored ways of making money.

One night, I asked, "Mom, would it be all right if I took on a paper route?"

She looked at me a bit astonished and questioned, "Will they let a girl have a paper route?"

I responded enthusiastically, "Yes, I've already asked them. Please, please, Mom. Can I?"

Rodney piped in, "What will my friends say?"

"Mom, if I have a paper route I can make two or three dollars a week. I can buy my own shoes," I said. Rodney looked over at mom and me. My Sunday church shoes were in good shape. But my school shoes had worn down soles with holes around the ball of the foot. They were stuffed with fresh cardboard daily. We all laughed and mom gave me permission to deliver papers.

Although I was ridiculed as I hauled around a big canvas bag with *The Ottawa Journal* stamped on it, I was able to buy the things I wanted with my own money.

One autumn day, I was hanging out in the schoolyard with friends. They all owned bicycles. Even my brother was given a bike for his thirteenth birthday from mom's hard earned savings.

I really wanted a bike. It would make my paper delivery easier, and I could take on a bigger route. I begged mom for a bike, but it was impossible. She just didn't have the money. Buying on credit was in its early stages, and I had a weekly income. I reckoned I could buy my own bike on credit and that's what I did. Filled with self-confidence, I went to B.F. Goodrich and made a proposal to the owner for one of his shiny new bikes.

"Hello," I said with authority. "I want to buy a bicycle on credit."

"You do?" He responded.

"Yes. I come from a very poor family, and I don't have a father, and my mother only had enough money to buy a bicycle for my brother."

He smiled. "I see. And how do you intend to pay for a bicycle?"

I beamed. "I have a paper route, and I make $3.50 a week."

The next afternoon I was riding a spanking new royal blue bicycle that cost $52.50 and I had a big basket installed to hold my newspapers. I was so enthused that I took on a short-lived early morning *Globe and Mail* delivery route and doubled my income. Every week I rode across the city to pay $2.50 a week for my bike.

Not only did the bike help my business, it gave me access to my favorite sport: horseback riding. My summer farm visits drew me to horses. For a time there was even an inner city riding stable at the Experimental Farm, easily accessed by public transportation. When it closed, the nearest stables were in Orleans, about fifteen miles east of Ottawa. I could easily bike there in about forty-five minutes. I would make a day of it, saving enough money for two rides, one in the morning and one in the afternoon.

But with all the stretching and bouncing going on, my jeans took the stress with a large bold rip down my backside center seam. Mom could only tell me I'd have to "make do." Sewing on a conventional patch was like having a pimple, so I opted to create a large red flannelette heart covering my backside, coordinated to match my red plaid shirt.

Cars honked as they witnessed my backside when I rode my bike. Others snickered, and the landlady was incredulous. But I don't believe anyone considered whether or not I was wearing ripped jeans.

The horses didn't care either if they were new or ripped jeans. I was usually thrown off. I was scratched all over my arms and face as the horses veered into uncharted paths that led inside the woods. Onward they galloped, taking me through trees with branches high enough for them to clear but not for me. In time, I learned proper riding form: boots back and down, not forward and down. Until then these horses knew an untrained kid and played with me. On a long stretch one day in a full gallop, the horse broke his stride and flipped me to his underside. Continuing his rapid pace, I felt like John Wayne as I desperately clung to the saddle. His galloping legs were just inches from my face. Clearly this horse was not going to come to my rescue by stopping. So I closed my eyes and let myself fall from the underbelly. His hooves flew over me, and as I landed, my big red heart patch plunked down into the middle of the only mud puddle on the trail.

Nothing deterred me from my love of horses, however, and I later advanced to English saddle riding and jumping. My landlady wished I'd give it up and made me keep my smelly clothes in the shed. While riding was my passion, it didn't consume all my time.

The love of an audience since my early days of presenting plays in grandma's yard was still with me. My junior school went only to grade six, so I had to change for grade seven. There I tried my hand at public speaking.

My heart was really in it. I loved the idea of being able to present ideas to a large group and worked hard to interest a diverse crowd of students, teachers and executives. I engaged mostly in topics from the encyclopedia: why we laugh and cry, why we have toes, etc. I won every time I spoke save once. But even with this success, grade seven and eight were psychologically difficult for me. In my old school I had recognition and respect for all my achievements. At the new school, I was virtually unknown except for a few old classmates. Bereft of foundations and of confidence, I often felt alone and isolated.

But with entering high school in 1953, I had other areas of which to concern myself. Conventional wisdom was that a girl should learn how to be a secretary, get a job, and marry the boss. Really. It was with fierce opposition that I bowed to my mother's wishes and attended the High School of Commerce. By everyone's account, the two-and-a-half years I spent there were a scholastic disaster. I wanted arts, and instead I had typing and shorthand classes. I excelled in penmanship, usually scoring over 100%, but I only once typed more than ten words per minute. That day, the teacher made a big to-do of it, presenting me with a chocolate bar.

However, I was still enthralled with stage. In my first year, I delivered my best speech ever - the life story of Ottawa Mayor Charlotte Whitten, Canada's first woman mayor of a major city, appointed in 1951. Rehearsing daily on the school bus, I heard unflattering comments such as,

"It's too boring. It has too many facts," or "There's too much detail." The students preferred to chant the unofficial school song,

"We go to Commerce, good girls are we.

We all have lost our virginity.

In the moonlight, we get hot.

And when you've got us, you've got a lot.

And when we give boys, we really give.

Dum deedee dum dum dum deedee dum

We are happy, we are gay

And we always go all the way."

What a backdrop that was. But indeed Ms. Whitten had a long list of contrasting ideas from feminism to her criticism of married women who worked. I knew if I could memorize the facts, I could deliver a speech with power.

The night of the speech came, and I stood nervously in front of a crowd who barely knew me. I started slowly and apprehensively, watching their faces as I spoke. The room hushed. The stories and facts about Ms. Whitten were interesting. They listened in awe. The speech concluded to generous applause. Ms. Whitten had once remarked, "Whatever women do, they must do twice as well as men to be thought of as half so good. Luckily it's not too difficult." I stood with pride as I took in the applause and inside shared this triumphant moment with her. I won the contest. But more importantly, I was appointed to the prestigious debating society, an honor I treasured deeply.

In the spring of 1955 I was invited to the Spring Prom. I was astonished at the invitation because I believed these social events were not for poor people. Ken Labelle was my charming escort, brother of my friend Shirley. I asked him why he wanted to go with someone like me to the prom.

With grace and aplomb he smiled and said, "Because I want to be with the prettiest girl there." While I was thrilled with the invitation and excited about going, inside it felt like I was a victim of a prank. Did his parents whom I adored, bribe him? Was it Shirley? Was he really going to show up? Was I still that little girl at grandma's house?

At fifteen, I was okay with guys - a flirt even. I knew guys liked me. But being called pretty and being invited to the school's biggest social event was alarming. I thought "pretty" belonged to girls with long hair, a nice smile, and nice teeth. I rarely smiled, had fine limp hair, lead-filled teeth, and a capped tooth in front. No matter, I was going.

My best friend's sister, Aline Macgregor, was excited to loan me a truly beautiful strapless blue prom gown with golden threads woven through it. Raiding her mom's jewelry box, I accessorized the dress with a three strand pearl necklace and pearl earrings. My hair was set in waves, my face powdered and my lips highlighted in soft pink. Ken was in awe when he picked me up. It was a magical night and a wonderful transformation of a girl dressed in lower income necessity into upper class finery. I walked straight and proud, and I left my insecurities behind. I chatted and giggled and held my own with a dignity I never knew I possessed. That "feel good" night like other highlights of my life would settle deep inside. On the surface, I would once again maintain my low self-esteem personality, feeling unloved. Later when I saw my prom picture I thought I looked awful and fat. I had big cheeks that earned me the nickname "Rod's fat sister."

Not long after the prom, however, I was sought out by some of the classier boys at school. I accepted an invitation to attend the opening night festivities for the Rideau Yacht Club. It was wonderful. However, I overheard my date tell someone that he was taking "Colleen Riley" to the opening. I was being referred to as pretty and wasn't it a coup that he was dating me. Well, for me, those remarks were offensive. Yes. I lived in a lonely world, and I wanted to be considered interesting and maybe smart but not pretty. I wanted to break the date but opted for a quirky revenge. I was dressed in a frilly white eyelet blouse and skirt when my date picked me up in his sporty car. Off we went. On entering the club, we were greeted by the traditional reception line. My date knew everyone. His arm holding mine, my date and I moved from person to person dressed in their stately nautical attire.

"I'd like to present Colleen Riley," my date said.

I smiled to each and said, "Good evening. So nice to be with you tonight." I delivered each greeting in a man's deep raspy voice similar to the one used in *The Exorcist*. It shocked everyone, but they were all gracious, giving a serious look to my date.

He bravely moved me along, too nervous to say a word. He never did call for another date. I often wondered about the scuttlebutt the next time he went to the club. Too bad for me though, I did like yacht clubs.

Like my social life, my academic life wasn't working out too well. In a row with the principal, I declared that I was going to quit school.

"Colleen," he said smugly. "You can't quit school. You're only fifteen years old."

THE LIFE AND TIMES OF A SINGLE WOMAN

"Oh no?" I questioned defiantly. "Watch me." With that, I picked up my books, cleared out my locker, and went home. Mom was at work when I arrived home. I was filled with excitement and also terror. There were such things as truant officers. Of course if I had a job offer, was in a single parent family, and mother would sign the papers, I could get approval to leave school. I rushed to the Bell Telephone office, filled out an application form, lied about my age (corrected it the following day when the official papers were signed), and was hired as a telephone operator. My income was $12.00 more a week than my mother was making. How could she say no? With two incomes we could make sure Rodney could get a college education.

It didn't look like I'd ever become a secretary and marry the boss, so mom signed the papers. I started work two days later. Within the first month, I bought the family a gray marbleized Formica and chrome five piece kitchen table set. We threw out a painted pine harvest table. I felt so proud. The new table was a peace offering for letting me quit school.

My final footsteps into a high school were at Lisgar Collegiate for a school dance. Rodney was in grade twelve there. As president of the Audio-Visual Club he worked with entertainers and introduced me to Rich Little. Rich monopolized my time, and we danced and talked the night away. Rich was well known around Ottawa because he had his own midnight radio show. He fascinated me because he was so interested in everything. He was possessed with a genuine curiosity about life. Although he was shocked when I told him I had been to nightclubs in Quebec (he believed that was naughty), he asked everything about them. Were they dark, dingy, and smoky? How did the people dress? Was everybody in couples? What time did they open? When did they close? And on and on . . . . We were radically different, but he left the dance promising he would play a song for me on the radio that night.

At 12:05 a.m. I tuned into his show.

"The next song is for Colleen Riley." I loved hearing my name on the radio. After that, Rich would call me every night before the show, and we would talk about life and the next song he was going to play for me. But as time went on, I needed my sleep. Besides, none of my friends were up late enough to hear my name, so I eased out of the calls. Rich Little went on to become one of entertainment's greatest impersonators.

My best friend at the time was Catherine "Kitty" Macgregor, a natural blond who was tall and pretty. Kitty lived a block away with parents whose words were laced with Scottish rrrr's. It was in their family library that I did all my research for public speaking.

Although it was a short term friendship, we met at age 11 and she moved to Toronto when I was 15, we had a strong bond and similar goals. Together we formed "The Trying Teens" with a small group of friends whose purpose was to help one family each Christmas. For the pre-selected family we made appropriate gifts and raised funds through caroling. On Christmas Eve, we would show up with gifts, turkey, peas, cranberries, and all the trimmings. For the two years we did it, it proved inspiring.

Kitty and I loved singing and when the song "Sisters" became a hit we decided to form a duet. We started singing everywhere we could: in school, in the park, on the bus. One day we received a phone call from a radio station asking us to perform at the ice sculpture show across from the war memorial in downtown Ottawa.

"Kitty," I said nervously on the phone. "A radio station wants us to sing at the ice sculpture show, live, on the air."

"What are we going to wear?" was her confirmation.

Hot, hot, hot in fashion was the circular felt skirt with appliqués of poodles and other décor topped with a twin sweater set. We looked great, but we forgot that it was winter. By the end of our three song set we were singing with shivers. It was marvelously thrilling, and we loved the recognition. That spring Kitty and her family moved to Toronto, and I looked for another singing partner.

My new closest friend was Adele Grace from Arnprior, a small town about 40 miles west of Ottawa. Adele was quite beautiful and possessed a grace and charm not common to the other friends I had at school. I can't recall with whom she lived in Ottawa, but on most Fridays her grandmother picked her up to spend the weekend in Arnprior. Adele often included me on these trips. They were terribly exciting, mostly because her grandmother, who was also quite beautiful, drove 80 miles an hour in her fancy beige car.

Adele's grandmother owned a hotel, which made me a guest of the owner.

On a beautiful summer morning in August 1956, Adele and I were sitting around the hotel lobby when she asked if I could help out her grandmother. The hotel wasn't too busy, and the kitchen staff had left until dinner. Someone booked an evening party that had to be catered.

"Could you help me prepare the food and decorate the room?" she asked. I loved being in the hotel kitchen. It was the first place I ever tasted aged cheddar cheese. When her grandmother served fresh apple pie, she let us slice our own wedges. Of course I would help.

Adele and I had a great time. We ran streamers and hung balloons. We worked with all the kitchen gadgets and prepared oval platters filled with sandwiches, egg dishes, vegetables, cheese trays and pickles. It was wonderful to work with an abundance of food, and we garnished everything with parsley and tomato.

With the task completed and inspected by her grandmother, we headed downtown to hang out and have some pop. Later that night, Adele and I were sitting around her suite. She started to giggle and asked, "Would you like to sneak down the backstairs and take a peek at the people at the party? Sometimes it can be really funny."

"Sure," I said. "Let's go."

Off we went down the back staircase with Adele whispering all the time, saying, "Keep your voice low." But we couldn't hear any sounds. No music. No talking. At the doorway, Adele opened it a crack only to see a dark room.

"I don't know what's going on," she said. "We better just walk in and see what's happening." Still hushed, Adele stridently moved forward with me close behind. In a flash, the lights turned on and about fifteen of Adele's friends yelled out, "Surprise. Happy 16th Birthday, Colleen." It was so much fun. Having worked all the day on the party, and it was all for me! Everyone brought me presents. It was unbelievable.

Shortly after the party, Adele moved away, and we lost contact. I missed her and Kitty a lot. But my life was always in motion.

A dance instructor discovered my interest in dancing after witnessing me one night at a club. He offered me a job for which he would train me. With a background in tap, ballet, ice skating, roller skating, and jiving, I was very keen to learn more. With his guidance in various dances (including the fox trot, samba, rumba, polka, tango and waltz), I picked up the steps quickly and was soon in a room filled with mirrors teaching students twice a week. This was something I enjoyed and stayed with for two years. I certainly liked the added income.

The school also ran modeling courses and offered me free lessons. I jumped at it. My posture was atrocious. Having developed a bust line earlier than most girls, I was embarrassed at my breasts. They pushed out my blouse, and I hunched forward to hide them. My mother and my aunts said that "Ten years old is too young to put her in a brassiere!" I discovered it was difficult to be confident with my shoulders slouching.

As my modeling lessons progressed, I was given two assignments, both wearing bathing suits. I was hired to appear as a stand up water skier in a parade. As luck would have it, on the day of the parade I awoke with my monthly menstrual cycle and was doubled over in pain. With bravado, I boarded the float. For an hour I smiled and waved graciously to the crowd while I was screaming inside. I swore never to do a parade again.

When I was called to do a fur coat fashion shoot on Parliament Hill a few months later, I thought "this is more like it." I readily accepted the assignment with nine other models. Backstage painted a different picture. Under the fur coat, we were to wear bathing suits, and the slimiest of men were on hand to do the fittings. My weak stomach felt an aching need to throw up. I was experiencing involuntary eye squinting. I hated being there but honored my commitment. The "cheesecake" photos were taken on the snow covered grounds of Parliament Hill. The models were donned in fur coats pulled to one side to show a profile bikini line. For me, modeling was now history. But I kept up the dancing.

My fancy footwork did not go unnoticed by Canadian hockey star Ralph Backstrom. We met at a Saturday night YMCA dance. Usually these dances were a yucky place to go, but at 16, my mother approved of the Saturday night outing. The guys were mostly Mounties with shaved heads, but on this night there were a few sports guys around. Of all things, Ralph was already infamous as Captain of the Hull-Ottawa Canadiens Juniors. He was a guy the girls swooned over, and of all things, he asked me to dance a polka. I was a dance instructor, so of course I could polka. After we had swung around the floor, he asked for my phone number. I remember the first time he called to invite me to a movie.

"What movie?" I asked.

"I don't know what movie. I just want to take you to a movie Saturday night."

"Well you're going to have to let me know what movie you want to take me to because if I don't like the movie then I won't want to go."

It wasn't the way things worked in the fifties. Girls were begging to say yes to Ralph for anything he wanted. My friends were astonished at the way I had treated him. He called me back with a movie proposal I liked and we started dating. Being the girlfriend of a Hockey Captain was fun. It came with a certain status. He also drove fabulous new cars (being part owner in an auto dealership). We dated for about six months until he was called to play hockey for the Montreal Canadiens in the National Hockey League. He eventually went on to the World Hockey League.

My mother's sister, Couranne, married Mike Abrams, a member of the Anka family. Our many family visits often included the Anka family. It was there that I met Bobby Anka, cousin to Paul the famous singer. I later joined Bobby's high school dance band as a duet singer, but the band was short lived for lack of bookings. I opted to try singing on my own.

"And our final contestant, ladies and gentlemen, is a young lady from Ottawa. Colleen Riley. Let's give her a round of applause," sounded the host at the Glen Lea Golf and Country Club in Hull, Quebec.

Brian Browne was on keyboards, and Paul Anka (who performed there regularly) was in the audience as I broke into my off-key rendition of "Roll Out The Barrel." It was hard to mess up, but I was so nervous that I screwed up all my songs. Still, I won. I was a young girl in a tight dress in a bar. For this, I won $25.00. I don't think anyone cared about my voice. Lusty men invited me to their table to show me the way to stardom. I didn't go. No agents tried to sign me.

Further opportunity had me singing in a week long gig at the Fairmont Club in Hull with another female singer. We billed ourselves as "The Plazettes," a name coined by our friends. It was a terrible place filled with an older crowd who loved to drink. Between sets an emissary would arrive at our table to invite us to get cozy with gray-haired and balding men whom they assured us could get us recording contracts. They all looked disgusting and glassy-eyed drunk. To the chagrin of management, we always refused.

"You can't just sit here in a nightclub, two women alone," The manager would tell us. Oh yes we could.

The next night we made sure our Ottawa friends were there to protect us. The guys were great. Since we had to do our last set at midnight, they organized two night shifts for the next five days. Singing was too complicated and soon went the way of modeling. There just wasn't much hope for two 18-year-old girls singing in a bar in Hull, and Ottawa was devoid of entertainment venues. By this time, I began writing poetry on any piece of paper around me. It was the first emergence of my writer within. With music still in my heart, I began to write lyrics.

The gang, the guys, my fan club, all loved my songs, and we would sing them in the car on our outings. It was encouraging to teach them my new lyrics which they sang with joy. For them, I gave one more performance at a hockey fund raising party. But the good times of being a member of the gang were coming to a close. My song writing, or any writing, was to go dormant while my life took on a more serious spin.

CHAPTER FIVE
LATE TEENS

As with most young women, life was confusing for me. I had no interest in marriage. I liked men, but I wanted to do other things with my life. I didn't see myself as a 1950s housewife doing dishes in a fancy apron. I listened to my Sarah Vaughan records with Rodney while we sat around the dinner table. Then we listened to his favorite record, Gene Krupa on the drums. We could only afford a couple of records, and poor mom had to listen to them over and over. Rodney and I would spar with each other by guessing the authors of famous quotations. Way ahead of me because of our different schooling, Rodney always won. That was until I discovered a quote by Ralph Waldo Emerson. With his usual pompous air, Rodney reamed off a quote. Rather than try to guess the author, I said, "Don't give me quotations. Tell me what you know." Rodney laughed but failed to name the author. Finally.

My dating was sporadic, and I was not skilled in my selection. One guy I dated took me to a picnic and dance on a Saturday night. It turned out he was a member of the Young Communist's Club, and the event was a combined recruiter's night. On Sunday afternoon two Mounted Police showed up at my home to investigate my participation with the group. The landlady went bananas, mom went bananas, and that ended that relationship. Another love interest was a tough guy who adored women. He started a fight with any guy who looked at him or me the wrong way. He always won, and I became Chucky's girl. He wanted to marry me and was saving his money to buy me a house. I did actually dream of a house of my own and may have gone for marriage. But one day he drove up in a new car he paid for in cash. It was the same cash put aside for the down payment on our house. It was time to get out of town.

I spent July of 1956 with Kitty in Toronto. If it was possible to fall in love with bricks, then I did. I fell in love with the bricks of Toronto's Union station. I can remember walking out the massive front doors and being compelled to touch each one. Once outside the station, my eyes caught sight of the magnificent Royal York Hotel located directly across the street. It was then the tallest building in Toronto. My inner voice murmured, "This is my city. This is where I'm going to live."

Kitty's family had a home on Primrose Avenue in the West End near a factory. Every morning at 7:30 a.m. marching band music blared through the factory's speakers while their employees headed to work. I'd spring up in sleepy amazement on the first few drumbeats which served as the family's call for breakfast. That was one of the few things I didn't like in Toronto.

My time there was filled with activities, family dinners and visiting all the usual tourist attractions. Compared to Ottawa, a quiet, government-dominated city, Toronto was filled with bright lights, theaters, restaurants, and a plethora of stores and bars on the famous downtown Yonge Street strip. Kitty's sister, Aileen, was outgoing and loved to get us all dressed up and out to eat in fine restaurants. That year marked the opening of Toronto's first outdoor restaurant amidst a barrage of adverse newspaper stories. Opened by a European entrepreneur, its idea was to bring a relaxed quality of life to Canada. Lunch was made fresh to order, taking at least thirty minutes to prepare. The restaurant was located in the heart of the fast-paced financial district, and this did not go over well with the locals. But for me, it only enhanced the love affair I was having with the city. The restaurant had shown me a glimpse of Europe and the fine cuisine I had only read about. Between it and the bricks of Union Station, I had touched a doorway to the world. I knew that I had to eventually move to Toronto.

Two years later I was there. I worked for Chase and Sanborn Coffee's head office and lived in my own third floor flat on Burnside Avenue. Kitty was married by then, so I started a horseback riding club at work and organized a social life around the club. Every Saturday, we rode at the Circle M Ranch about an hour outside the city.

Circle M was located on an old movie site near Kleinburg and filled with incredible visuals. The small town facades of Kleinburg's main street had been created for western movies and old scripts were lying around for us to ham around with. Dangerous, narrow paths took us around the steep sides of high hills, and there were small bodies of water to ride through or go around. Sharing our picnic lunches, a group of around eight people made up my new world of friends. But I missed my mother, and eight months later I returned to Ottawa, vowing to move back to Toronto when I was older.

Inside my home in Ottawa, the early mornings would find my mother calling out, "Esterella, Esterella. Lather up and have some cafetoria."

We loved having our morning coffee together, and mom had her own way of making life fun. My gang, the chips-and-gravy-and-cherry coke gang, hung out at a restaurant called the Esterel on Sparks Street. Hence my nickname Esterella. Filled with cushy booths, that was our spot everyday from 4:00 p.m. One could show up anytime after 4:00 p.m. and find a friend, deciding the night's activities and who would ride in who's car. When all together, there were about 25 of us, but the core group was about eight or nine. These were the friends who went out every night of the week. That included me.

Our weekly routine was to go out from Tuesday to Saturday. Sunday was family time. Monday was wash, iron, and get ready for the other weeknights. I was a finicky person. Every piece in my dresser was meticulously laid out. All accessories were placed in a neat pile, the scarf, the gloves, and the coordinated flower. Every item of clothing was ironed to perfection, and every pair of panties was pressed and neatly folded. Some say this detail comes with Virgo territory. It may when you're young.

One of our main haunts was the Chaudierre Club (or the Chaud as it was called), across the bridge in Hull, Quebec. A huge nightclub, it was down the road from the Glen Lea where I had sung. The lure of the Chaud was the downstairs dance bar. It was a true rock'n'roll spot where we jived, twisted, and bopped to tunes like "Rock Around The Clock," "Don't Be Cruel," "The Purple People Eater," "Cathy's Clown," "It's All In the Game" and many other great songs. Although I had various boyfriends, I hung out with the gang where I felt safe and always had a good time.

Occasionally we treated ourselves to a nightclub show upstairs at the Chaud or shot over to the Glen Lea. Both featured big stars like the Four Aces, Connie Francis and Earl Grant.

Late one night when returning home from the Chaud, concerned that our driver had too much to drink and was driving too fast, I asked to be let out of the car. We had just left the parking lot on a warm summer night, and we were on Aylmer Road heading for the bridge to Ottawa. I figured I could walk over the bridge and catch a bus in Ottawa.

As I walked in the dark of night alongside the highway, it felt good to be away from the dangerous driving. Soon enough however, Dominique, a bartender from the Chaud, pulled alongside and asked if I wanted a lift. He was polite and concerned about me walking on the highway alone, and appeared sober, so I accepted the ride.

He was quite charming. Born in Italy, he and his family had recently moved to Canada, and he barely spoke English. Fair-haired and green-eyed, he didn't look Italian. He had a cleft chin and was quite handsome. At nineteen, I was a year older than him, but when he asked me out for a picnic the following day, I accepted.

Dominique was playful and even in his broken English he could make me laugh. Having two months severance pay from my last job, I took the summer off. My days were free as were his, and we eventually saw each other every day. He drove a trendy '55 Chevy, and everyday we headed out of town to a beach, to picnic or to make love. We were falling in love, and I was so excited about him. We drove to Fort Coulounge, so he could meet my family. Most of our dates began or culminated at his aunt's house. Mrs. Persi was joyful and energetic, and our visits all took place in her kitchen where she prepared fabulous Italian dishes.

"You must eat something," she would say, a smile embracing her Italian accent while she looked straight into my eyes.

Her sister, Dominique's mother, abhorred our relationship. There were no smiles in her house, and she would tear into Dominique in Italian as soon as we entered.

As the end of summer moved to the dawn of September, I began my days with a sick stomach and found myself pregnant. I was thrilled with the news and anxious to tell the man I loved.

"Dominique," I looked into his soft warm eyes. "I have something to tell you."

"What is it?" he queried back as we sat on my mother's sofa that September day.

Ecstatic, my face beamed, my mouth smiled, my joyful soul spoke, "I'm pregnant."

His eyes hardened, and he shifted around. First he got mad, but soon he melted and touched my stomach.

With caring, he said, "That's our little baby in there."

Those were the last decent words he would say to me.

CHAPTER SIX
SINGLE PARENTING

By the fall of 1960, I had turned 20 years old, was single, and two months pregnant. Dominique offered me a confining life, telling me that we would live in his house with his family where I would learn to be an Italian wife. I would have the car but never be able to use it unless his mother was with me. There would be no milkman coming to the door. I could shop for milk and anything else with his mother. Notwithstanding that his mother did not speak English, she despised me. She wanted an Italian woman for a daughter-in-law. At the times he would be home from work, he intended to keep me under surveillance.

Dominique changed. He was excessively jealous and accused me of flirting and having affairs. When he arrived at my apartment to pick me up (where I lived with my mother and brother), he entered all the rooms and looked in the closets trying to catch me with a man stashed away. We were all stunned. I was fearful. I was carrying his child. I loved him. I wanted to please him.

"Now that you're pregnant, you can have sex with any man and not have to worry," he said. I sat brokenhearted, looking at the man with whom I was in love. I wondered where my friend was: the lover who made me laugh, the one who couldn't wait to see me everyday, the one who gave me a gold plated heart locket for his picture. Nothing I said stirred his heart. I was terribly confused.

Every time we went into a restaurant, he accused me of flirting with someone - anyone. If I didn't stare into his eyes every minute, if I turned for one moment, I was accused of making eyes at a man across the room. As soon as we were alone, he would pick on me.

"You're a slut. You want to fuck every man you see."

I recoiled and asked for understanding. "Please, Dominique. I only love you. I don't want anyone else."

"I saw the way you looked at that man," he responded. "In ten years your life will be finished from all the fucking. You'll be a broken-down whore."

Where was it all coming from?

Standing beside him at the cash, if I looked up at a male cashier, I was maliciously chastised. Confused and frightened, I was in the grip of a serious depression. Unaware of my mental state, I continued to see Dominique and endure his abuse until a potential tragedy occurred.

We were driving in the country one afternoon and stopped for gas. The attendant was someone I used to work with at a company that had since gone bankrupt. The company, Edge Limited, was an industrial plumbing and heating organization where I was the secretary/receptionist and the only female on staff. I had worked there for about a year and knew everyone. I felt bad about all the lay-offs, especially the married men who had wives and children.

The trustees made me a generous offer to work with them until they wound down the affairs of the business. It was that funding that provided me the summer months off.

It was natural to say hello to the attendant, inquire as to how he was making out, and ask about other employees. It was polite conversation but not in the eyes of Dominique.

It was a bright sunny day in October as we drove off onto the highway. In my innocence, I was pleased to hear good news about former associates and was dwelling on those warm thoughts when the iceberg hit.

"So you fucked all those men! You're nothing but a filthy whore," he screamed at me. My head dropped, the tears welled up, and the confusion and pain began again.

"Dominique, I never slept with those men I asked about. I used to work with them," I pleaded, filled with the naiveté of thinking that once he knew the truth everything would be all right.

"How about this one and that one?" he mimicked. "You whore. You're nothing but a whore. You'll always be a whore. I know you fucked them all." He heated up, his voice raised, and he stepped harder on the gas. My head was exploding.

"Stop. Stop yelling at me," I yelled back.

His dirty mouth continued to spew the filth of his thoughts. He was pompous, arrogant, and commanding. I recoiled in fear, feeling it was never going to end. I had no defense because it was all in his mind. I felt there was no way out. I had to stop the abuse. My heart was pounding, my temperature was rising, and my thinking was muddled. He wouldn't stop yelling. I decided to leap out of the speeding car. I didn't care if it meant my death. I just didn't know how else to get away from his anger.

I reacted swiftly. In seconds, my hand reached the door handle. I opened the door, and I jumped.

"This is it. It's over," I thought as I rolled down the roadside gully. In fleeting seconds, I looked at the blades of grass now inches from my eyes and reasoned that they were my last look at this earth. It wasn't a deep gully, and I reached the bottom in a daze. I was alive. I looked around and Dominique was coming toward me. I thought of the baby. I didn't know if I could move. Covered in guilt, Dominique picked me up in his arms and carried me to the car. I felt drugged. I was groggy and felt nothing mattered. He drove me to a hospital emergency room where they put me on a bed. I waited with a glazed stare, afraid I had hurt the baby. Dominique, finally, was silent. With my eyes swollen and red from crying, I was a mess. My hair was tossed, and I had grass stains on my disheveled clothes. An intern examined me. Then a doctor took me to a private office where he insisted on hearing the whole story.

"You and the baby are fine, but you have some serious problems to work out. You need to do some hard thinking on your own. I advise you not to see Dominique for at least a week. I'm sure you'll find the right answers."

Not long after on a fine fall day, I sat in the park holding my tummy and took account of what was happening. I was pregnant. If I had an abortion, I would miss the baby I had already come to love. If I kept the baby, I would probably have to raise it on my own. I wanted to be a writer. I had already written songs and poems, and I had a desire to eventually write books. I knew my time commitments in both working and motherhood would preclude the chance to establish a writing career.

Inside me, a tiny infant was depending on me for a life, for good health - including good mental health. Could I be strong enough, smart enough, and committed enough to provide the right environment?

That afternoon in the park I became a mother. I was a free spirit, and marriage to Dominique would be like putting a bird in a cage. I hated the vision of the oppression my child would have to live under if I married him. I decided to go ahead with the pregnancy and raise the child on my own. I pacified my writer's soul by telling myself that I was young and could be a writer later. It was time to put my dreams on hold and take responsibility for the situation I was in. With a new found strength I told Dominique that I did not want to marry him and that I could keep and raise the baby on my own. He was stunned at my assertive and authoritative manner. He had only seen me as an adoring, loving, and passive girlfriend. He called my mother a few times to ask if I was going to sue him for support. He and I never spoke directly again. I began eating healthy foods and contacted the Children's Aid Society to guide me through my mission.

Soon I was living with a family as a helper to a mother of four. They lived in a modern bungalow, and every Saturday night drove me to town to spend Sunday with my own family. It looked like I was going to make it, and I centered my thoughts on motherhood. I had a lovely bedroom furnished in white wormwood with a loveseat, a library, and a radio. The kids were great, and the family was loving. Just as I was settling in and feeling thankful for my blessings, it began.

"Colleen, don't you dare keep the baby. You give it up the moment it is born," Great Aunt Margaret would scream into the phone at me. Every week she called, sometimes suckering me into conversations that always led to her great anger about how I was destroying the family.

Worse than that, she would call my mother at work and pressure her to deal with me. But both mother and my brother stood firmly behind me and my decision. They told family members that what I did would be my decision. Their support shone brightly for me. I remember the look in Rodney's eyes when I told him I made my decision to go ahead with the pregnancy. He was surprised, and yet he seemed pleased.

"You're going to have a baby?" he said.

"Yes I am. Sometime in early May," I replied.

"And you're not getting married, and you're going to raise him on your own?" he continued repeating what I had just told him. And we talked on for the afternoon. Brother and sister; finally getting to know each other.

Aunt Lillian, my mother's sister, was another main detractor who telephoned me regularly. Her calls were more loving, but the message was the same.

"Colleen," she would start in her broken English, "if you keep the baby no man will ever love you. They will call you a whore. No man will ever marry you. It's not fair to your mother. You should give the baby up." She called every few weeks with the passion of her message intensifying as the moment of birth drew close. "Are you sure you want to be known as a whore? You still have time to change your mind," she would ramble on. None of it mattered: not all the yelling, not the predictions that the sanctity of my life would be desecrated. I was no longer a child simpering under my grandmother's loathing. I was entering nature's strongest force – that of motherhood. The words of sharp tongues evaporated like snowflakes on the warm breath of love.

Nothing was ever more moving than holding my child in my arms for the first time. A force of incomparable love filled me as I examined each finger, his adorable face, and the strands of hair heading in every direction. For the first time in months, I wished Dominique were with me to share the great joy. Tears streamed down my face as I felt the love and made silent promises of responsible

65

mothering. Robert Lawrence Riley arrived at 1:30 p.m. on May 3, 1961 at 7 lbs. 1 ounce. I began my journey.

After careful consideration, I left Dominique's name off the birth certificate. His abuse terrified me, and I was afraid to keep a connection. I also decided to be Robert's sole supporter, never asking Dominique for money. I didn't close the door on giving Dominique visiting rights, but he preferred to keep his distance. He was informed about Robert and I by his aunt, Mrs. Persi, who always had a loving open door for us. We visited her frequently over the years. She was our tie to the family.

Great Aunt Margaret refused to acknowledge Robert's existence and eventually cut me from her will. Aunt Lillian was the first to send a gift, a luxurious baby blue stroller, and she offered whatever help I needed.

At birth, Robert was turned over to the Children's Aid Society to be cared for until I was financially stable. In cases where an unwed parent needed financial support, gaining aid required sanctioning by a judge. The day after I was released from the hospital, I made an appearance in court with my aid worker. I sat nervously as my aid worker stated my case.

Then the judge spoke, "Many young women come before me in this court," he said, "wanting with all their heart to keep their child. In most cases I do not recommend they be allowed. The reason is that most of them are not capable of responsible parenting. We end

66

up with the children when they are six months or a year old and much harder to adopt."

I was so nervous. I believed he was setting me up for rejection.

"In your case however, with everything I have heard here today, I feel confidant the baby will be looked after in a good home. I am recommending custody."

My social worker and I were beaming.

He added kindly, "I note here that you will require financial assistance for six months and that assistance is granted. And, my child, should you run into any problems, remember that we are here to help you."

Whew! The decision meant that as soon as I had a job and a furnished home for the two of us, I could take Robert home.

Robert was placed in St. Joseph's Adoption House where I was able to visit him once a week for two hours. On every visit, the nurse would tease me about how many parents wanted to adopt him. Panic engulfed me, but it prompted a vigorous campaign to get an income and a nice home.

Before long I had a receptionist job for a building contractor, and within two months I found a flat. Located in the back of a converted house, I had the main floor back room complete with a kitchen sink located in the hall closet under the stairs and a private back staircase to the back bedroom. The main floor washroom was shared with one other family living on the same floor.

Every payday brought with it the joy of running to the Salvation Army to buy furniture. Within a short time, I had the place fully furnished, complete with crib and bassinette. My handy sewing skills allowed me to buy mounds of fabrics from which I made drapes, matching cushions, and fabric throws to coordinate it all. The wood furniture was all painted black with gold trim.

Within four months, I brought Robert home. It was Labor Day weekend, giving us three free days to establish our new world. My neighbor next door with her own four children would start baby sitting on Tuesday morning. Every night, as she handed me my beautiful baby, she also handed over a bag of dirty diapers. The washing machine was conveniently squeezed into the cupboard beside the sink. The swish, swash of the washer was the background dinner music for Robert and me. He didn't mind. My world was coming together. My soul, however, still begged to be heard.

****

Penned Moments Revisited

Just as a man, who has been abandoned for days in a desert cries out to the deaf sands around him, "Water. Water." So my unspoken thoughts cry out to me. I, selfish of my time, smother their means of survival: my pen.

My father in 1939.
About six months later he
died.

1943 Mom in a giant sleeved
muskrat coat and me
looking a bit confused.

Fun times at 3 yrs. old in
Fort Colounge with my
French Canadian family.

My cousin Rose May and
me with the family dog in
Fort Colounge.

Mom sitting in a chair we had just covered in chintz. About 1955.

At my high school prom Spring 1955

Modeling was not for me.

I loved Monroe posing

WHL Hockey player Ralph Backstrom when we were dating in 1957.

Me with my son at his Christening.

Mom with Robert and fifties drapes.

Robert at Mosport in either Mario Andretti's or A.J. Foyt's racing car.

Robert on his first day of school, 1966.

Me and Robert in Mrs. Persi's home.

Robert with his favorite bus.

I was teaching Robert the song "Do your ears hang low" over on Center Island.

My friend Kitty
(Katherine) Macgregor.

My friend Adele from
Arnprior.

Sam, The Record Man,
Sniderman, is the first to
receive a copy of our record,
Keeping You on my Mind. ©

By 1956 I was working and
buying my own clothes. I
loved this coat.

At age 17, I was Chucky's girl.

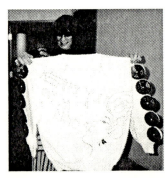

Marilyn Brooks made Robert a special "Keeping You on my Mind" © shirt with record labels up the arms.

The horseback riding team I put together in 1959, at the Circle M ranch.

Yikes. Those 60's glasses I wore to Mosport park.

Mosport Park, corner one, late 1960's.

CHAPTER SEVEN
OFF TO TORONTO

Many new forces were at work as I started life as a single parent. I loved being a mother and found joy in everything from the diapers to an hour of play after dinner. Robert was a wonderful baby, gentle and without aggression. Every day was a renewal of the great love I felt at his birth.

Within a few months, shifting my focus from single parent to head of the household, I sought a better paying job. I landed one as purchasing agent at Carleton University, bringing in $10.00 more a week. I now earned in excess of $50.00 a week. Within eight months, I bought my first car, a white Morris, for cash. Well, almost cash. There was a professor at Carleton University who found a tin mine in Quebec. Many at the university had made a pile of money in the stock market over this mine. With eight hundred dollars of my savings in the bank ready for a car purchase, I wrote a check for nearly all of it to invest in the mine. I hoped to make a few dollars before the car deal closed. Instead, the stock plummeted, I sold fast, and I salvaged 60% of my investment. I signed for my first bank loan to pay off the car.

Owning a car was liberating, but since I bought it from a friend it didn't come with instructions. Without technical knowledge, I blew up the engine in four months. No one told me that I had to check the oil and the water. I thought all it needed was gas. I took it on a 250 mile trip from Ottawa to Toronto for a job interview and did the car in. But the trip itself was successful. I landed a job. It was all thanks to the man I was dating.

Dennis Fournier and I had met shortly after Robert was born, and he came to be my mentor. He was a much sought after bachelor sporting a 1961 long yellow Cadillac and a 25' yacht. I was flattered when he asked me out. Of course, I felt he would cast me aside as my aunts had warned once he knew I had a child out of wedlock.

"Are you kidding me?" he responded. I had started my story with how I knew he would never want to see me again when I told him about myself. "I meet so many girls who don't have one ounce of your caring and your courage. Your aunts are wrong. You're not a whore. I'm in awe of you." Wow. I was filled with determination. Dennis was my reinforcer. He was fearless and always enthusiastic.

"When you're out with Robert in the stroller and you meet someone," he directed, "look them right in the eye and say, 'This is my son'. Be proud of what you are doing, bringing him up."

His love and support taught me strength. I had never known anyone who stood his ground without fear. The support I received from Dennis fortified me for the move to Toronto, and it ultimately created the demise of our relationship. Once in Toronto, I embraced the feeling of independence again. It was unfair to continue seeing him on weekends. I wrote a letter breaking things off, but I never let go of the strength he taught me to believe in. I was told he married a few years later.

When I decided to move to Toronto in 1962, I scoured the classifieds of a Toronto newspaper in search of a good paying job. Secretaries and the like were only paid $35.00 to $40.00 a week. However, the "Male Help Wanted" ads for seemingly simple jobs offered $70.00 to $80.00. Heck, I was the head of the family, so I wrote a three page letter to one firm on why a female would be better for the job. They advertised for a cost accountant in a steel and lumber yard paying $70.00 a week. Since the job entailed wearing a hard hat and physical contact with steel and lumber, my letter amused the executives. But it also impressed them, and they arranged an interview. Of course, telling them I had only one appointment left for the upcoming weekend also helped. In fact, they were the only company I wrote. Motherhood was calling out my chutzpah! I was hired to work in accounting for their estimating and detailing division. Well, I did also imply I was a whiz in accounting. Could Fred Astaire dance?

Having paid my dues in Ottawa for over a year by proudly walking my son in his stroller along Bank Street while nodding to the curious and having faced my family issues, I felt free to move to my chosen city and make a new start. The bank funded a newish car, and I packed it with all our belongings. We were off to Toronto on a bright summer morning on August 31, 1962. At sixteen months old, Robert sat with his beloved blue wool blanket in the front seat while the back was filled roof high with boxes, an ironing board, and a broom handle that stretched out the back window. The Beverly Riley-billies were on their way to a new life.

We lived in the Toronto suburb of Scarborough, an expansion community comprised mostly of bungalows built on large lots and high rise apartment complexes. I was saddled with car payments and high rent. My great new income was stretched to the max. We did, however, live in a large two-bedroom apartment. Our furnishings were sparse, and I remember telling the superintendent that a truck would be coming from Ottawa in a few weeks with our furniture. Of course it never came.

On weekends, with lunches packed, we went for rides in the country. We looked at farm animals or went on winter walks in northland forests.

We didn't have a telephone and barely knew anyone. This made the nights long and lonely for a 22-year-old woman. But the big picture - my own apartment, my own son, my right to be me - gave me the strength I needed.

One highlight of that time for me was buying a box of Tintex fabric dye for twenty-five cents to re-color the bedspreads and drapes. I also tore a dress apart and restyled it. I made all Robert's clothes and gave him a British look with coordinated vests and brown velvet collars on camel-colored coats.

Although my job paid well, and I was grateful to the company, it was boring. There were no young people around. The following year I jumped at the opportunity to work as a Girl Friday for Grant Clark, the Canadian Racing Car Champion and British Motor Company automotive dealer. I was also paid $5.00 more a week, and that made a big difference.

Grant's office was always ablaze with excitement. Mechanics would plunk the guts of a new gearshift on my desk and say, "Look at this, Colleen. Isn't beautiful!"

Grant himself was charismatic and known as the Don Juan of the track. As his right hand confidante, I was the sympathetic ear to many a broken-hearted girl. Most women who dated him once begged to see him again, and I fielded the stream of phone calls.

On weekends from spring to autumn, racing events were staged at Mosport Park. Being part of the champion's team had great status in the pits. Grant's charm appealed to everyone. He possessed a rare engaging personality. Men admired him, and women adored him.

For two-year-old Robert and me, our trips to Mosport were true respite. We headed out at 5:00 a.m. with a hibachi, food, and a pop cooler and set up outside corner one of the track - our favorite spot. After breakfast, we sauntered over to the pit, pinned on our heavy-duty badges, and hung out with the likes of Mario Andretti, Richard Petty, Bobby and Al Unser, Bill Brack, and all the greats.

Andretti took Robert for spins in his racing car, and singer Keely Smith insisted Robert have lunch with her.

Back at the dealership, Grant was always kind to me. He always gave into my whims to drive special cars we had for sale on the lot. I drove everything from a Porsche to a Carmen Ghia to an Ogle. Once he let me drive a Ferrari but only around the block. The car I loved most, however, was the long, sleek Jaguar XKE which I could occasionally keep overnight. I would open it up on the curvaceous Don Valley Parkway after midnight, practicing all I had learned from observation and from reading books on racing. It was an awesome feeling of power. The newly built Parkway was almost barren at that time of night.

Andre Coffman, editor of the race car publication called *Track and Traffic*, offered me poet laureate status at her newspaper. A non-paying assignment, I was asked to write a racing poem for each monthly issue. I wrote for two issues before the paper was sold off and turned into a magazine. Toronto took on a new color and within a short time I knew at least 50 people and had developed friendships within the racing world.

Some years later for me, I had an incredible relationship with an Ottawa poet, singer, and guitarist, Bill Hawkins. He had recently released a book of poetry *Shoot Low Sheriff. They're Riding Shetland Ponies*. He had just moved to Toronto and was hip and happening. He worked on the floor of the Sam the Record Man store and lived in a campy third floor flat with a walk up fire escape. It was located on Gerrard Street East in the trendy row that housed the Village Bookstore, The Prince of Serendip Antiques and the Tate Gallery.

Bill was married, but he left his wife in Ottawa to pursue a creative life in Toronto.

I remember the night we met. We were hanging out at a friend's house. He sang and played guitar for me, doing a few joints in between. I loved his music and was inspired to write a poem on the spot. He was so cool and casual - so part of the scene.

He was quickly adopted into the poets' circle. We hung out at the Bohemian Embassy on Nicholas Street, a literary gathering space for many of Canada's leading poets. Every Friday night we went to the Pilot Tavern on Yonge Street where I emptied my purse on the table. Together we counted the change I had thrown in during the week. It was used to pay for the beer. Bill was always too poor.

At times when I had a late night baby sitter, Bill and I frequented an after-hours spot, The Club Bluenote. It was just around the corner from Bill's apartment. A cliquey place, it was the gathering spot for R&B musicians and attracted performers who were in town on gigs. It opened at 1:00 a.m., and the jam sessions went on until the wee hours, nurturing the true depths of soul and R&B. The sounds of "Georgia On My Mind" would wail on into the night as performers left their professional persona aside and "got down."

Incredibly drawn to each other, Bill and I would hug and hold and sway to the music. But my fear of pregnancy precluded a sexual relationship. Strangely, I wasn't sparked with jealously when Bill told me that the only way he could continue was if he had affairs with other women. None of it took away from the nights of literary joy at poetry readings or the long psychological and philosophical talks we had about life. After a year or so, Bill returned to Ottawa, and his wife. He released a second book, *Ottawa Poems,* to great response. With guitar in hand, he sang songs into the night in the Ottawa clubs. Then I lost track of him.

After Bill left, I had time on my hands. I took on small bookkeeping jobs. The extra income led me to a great part time job. I met Ottawa entrepreneur Lenny Alexander at a party in Toronto, and he asked me to open the Toronto branch of the Lenny Alexander Booking Agency for nightclub bands. Ron Scriber owned Bigland Booking Agency and was Toronto's booking power house. But Lenny still saw an opportunity to make a few bucks by rotating acts like Little Caesar and The Counsels from one city to the other. Soon after I opened the Toronto office, I began booking acts like Luke Gibson and The Kensington Market into clubs such as The Purple Onion and The Penny Farthing. The music industry performed its fresh acts on the two block strip of Yorkville Avenue where the infamous Riverboat was located. It was owned and operated by Bernie Fiedler who had a keen ear for music and a smart mind for business. He knew how to promote and made his club one of the most sought after places to perform. Record companies flocked to him to negotiate record launches for their new artists. A stint at the Riverboat could produce an overnight success story.

The heavy concentration of clubs in Yorkville meant one could simply walk down the street and meet, at one time or another, nearly everyone in the music industry, from artists to managers to booking agents to record company executives to promotion people. Deals were done from a sighting and a wave.

My Yorkville office was across the hall from Rafael Markowitz. Rafael was then managing George Oliver, the Blue Eyed Prince of Soul and the Mandella with Dominic Troiano. There was always a lot of screaming going on in that office, but the end result produced two of Canada's best acts. Rafael was to later become my first client when I opened my press and publicity business.

A club on Asquith Avenue became my favorite haunt. Julian Burns opened an incredible jazz music venue in a quaint two storey turn-of-the-century building and called it the First Floor Club. Julian and I were buddies from the first time we met. We saw each other every day for lunch or coffee, and I was at the club as often as baby sitters and time permitted.

Jazz musicians were having a rough time in the 60's and could barely afford the gas to get to Toronto. Julian or an emissary was consistently at the U.S./Canadian border with a delivery of food and gas money. Then, one day, Julian disappeared. Poof! I never heard from him again. Some say he moved to San Francisco. Some say he was involved in drug dealing. Nobody knew anything for certain. I was sure he would call. He never did.

In the fall of 1964, no longer the Canadian champion, my boss Grant Clark was arrested for selling hot cars. The dealership collapsed. The doors were bolted closed. I was out of work. A few days later a loving note and a check for $50.00 arrived by mail from my mother. It was her whole week's pay. It was just enough to get me through until my office skills were sought by Barry Rosenberg. He was an up and coming racing driver who had just opened Canada's first Ferrari dealership, Citation Motors.

Barry had style. The Ferraris were showcased in a wonderful pie-shaped showroom with twenty foot ceilings and huge semi-circular windows. Barry's second storey office overlooked the sales floor. Not too tall and with a slight build, Barry had a dark complexion, deep brown eyes, and thick black hair. With impeccable taste, he arrived every day wearing finely tailored suits and jackets, Italian ties, and a winning smile.

My working hours became a little easier when I found Anna and Paulo Portelli. They answered an ad I had placed for a sitter. Anna was an Italian housewife and mother of two small children. She liked Robert right away. She and Paulo lived in a house on a quiet street a few blocks over, and I was comforted to know Robert was in such a loving environment. For the first time, I didn't have to worry about working late. Anna was glad to keep Robert for dinner or even overnight.

Settling into my new home and job, and working with Barry was just the antidote I needed from the shock I felt after Grant's arrest. Barry had gathered a team of enthusiastic employees, including some of Grant's former racing crew. Mosport and the pits were still fun, and Barry with all his flash kept life interesting. I took a giant step and bought a new white MG Midget sports car with a red interior.

In this relaxed atmosphere, I called my boss "Barry Ferrari." We were a hardworking team, and there were always pranks going on. The best prank was a call from a smooth talking young lady who invited Barry to lunch.

"Citation Motors," Barry answered the phone one night in the showroom.

He listened for a moment, "No, I'm not really Italian but some people say I look like Pedro Rodrigues. Pedro was a famous race car driver from Puerto Rico.

He listened and then blushed, "Really. You've been in the showroom. You've seen me?" She charmed the pants off him, and he went for it.

"Well how about lunch?" Barry asked. His eyes rolled up, and he grinned. "Oh so you want to play hard to get?" He was now radiating.

"So then why don't you have lunch with me?" He began to nod his head in a yes. "Okay, so when?"

After the phone call Barry was sailing.

"Colleen, this incredible, dynamic woman, who is very hard to get, is meeting me for lunch. I'm meeting her tomorrow at noon in front of the museum. She's going to wear a white blouse and a navy skirt." I was sure Barry was trying to impress me because of my association with Grant, the Don Juan of the track. Whatever it was, it was all machismo.

The next day Barry arrived in a five hundred-dollar brocade ensemble. He was dressed.

"Open the showroom window." He demanded.

"Barry," I said, "You're not taking the Ferrari for the lunch date, are you?"

With arrogance he responded, "Of course I am."

By this time I was laughing. "But Barry, there's only 54 miles on this car." The car was a beautiful white Ferrari 2+2 American.

Sliding into the car, he responded, "I'm off."

As Barry approached the museum area, he couldn't get within blocks. There were cars and people everywhere and parking was a nightmare. His dream of wheeling up in the new Ferrari was destroyed, but he was still determined. He found a parking lot and walked through the thousands of people to the front of the museum.

At twelve noon that day, the Queen Mother was arriving. In her honor fifty British airline stewardesses were lined up on the steps of the museum all wearing white blouses and navy skirts.

Barry was laughing wholeheartedly as he recounted the story. No one, during my time there, claimed responsibility.

But Toronto was not yet ready for fast-paced expensive cars, and the Ferrari dealership was in trouble. I looked for greener pastures and landed a job in office administration with one of the city's most creative public relations agents, Frank Duckworth of the Duckworth Office. Frank had a progressive company that was soon bought out by advertising giant Baker, Lovick, BBDO. I moved with them into swank new offices downtown where we were renamed Rapport Public Relations. The move gave Frank the money he needed to buy a spectacular home on Fallingbrook Road at the edge of Scarborough Bluffs. Complete with swimming pool, his home became an extension of the office. Clients were entertained there often.

With clients like Eastern Air Lines, Gilby's Distillers, Bick's Pickles, there was always one promotion after another with far too much social drinking. Of course, it was fun. But it was not a lifestyle I wanted with a son waiting to see me at the end of the day. I undertook the task of managing a staff of fifteen and was quickly promoted to the holding company where I was groomed for comptroller. This entailed moving around to various departments to learn the advertising business inside and out.

When I hit the creative department it was disastrous. The men were after the women all the time. Being paid huge sums of money, these creative giants were arrogant and threatening. I was 26, blonde, curvy, and driving my white MG sports car. The guys were always hitting on me. I had my own world and own friends, but they wanted to hit the bars every night at 5:00 p.m.

"Colleen," Bruce Tyler said one day. "If you don't start saying yes to our invitations we're going to black ball you." Bruce was one of the arrogant creative staff that management handled with kid gloves. That was it. I was out of there with a hope and a prayer that a job was waiting at the end of my two weeks notice.

Taking chances doesn't always pay off. My need to have sufficient funds to survive found me on Spadina Avenue in the heart of the rag trade. I was hired as a bookkeeper for an Italian import house. The work was tedious and the atmosphere was boring. It wasn't long before I slipped into a depression. I felt my grandmother's presence. In rough times she was there with her messy, stringy, gray hair, thin craggy face, and pursed lips espousing her disgust at me.

The joyful image I had of myself bopping around in my sports car turned into the drudgery of just having to drive to work. Now when I was at Mosport, a race was just a race. I wanted so much to climb out of this state of mind, but instead I had to face an even greater challenge.

The hospital called me one morning.

"Mrs. Riley," the woman said. "This is the Sick Children's Hospital calling. Your son has had an accident."

"An accident? What's wrong with him? What happened?" I screamed with tears rushing to my eyes.

"He was playing with matches and has a few burns," she said in soft tones. "Nothing too serious, but we do need you to come down to the hospital."

On the drive there I kept repeating her words, "Nothing too serious." I felt panic and calm . . . then panic and fear.

Nothing prepared me for the sight I was to see. I thought I would be signing some forms and taking Robert home.

The attendant put me in a gown, put gloves on me, placed a mask over my face, and led me into the burn ward. Lying on a bed was my beautiful five year old son with 25% of his body covered in burns. His right side from the waist right up to his chin, his shoulder, and his arm were all a glowing mass of liquid silver.

"Nothing too serious." I screamed as the tears hit my eyes.

The doctor led me into the corridor. "Your son has suffered second and third degree burns. He struck a match and the whole book of matches lit up and caught fire to his shirt." Her voice was gentle but it held authority.

My tears continued to pour. With turned down, quivering lips I asked, "What's going to happen to him? How long will he be here?"

She turned her head to one side and then back to me. "We're not sure. Maybe eight weeks. Maybe 12 weeks. Some of the burns are deep, and he is going to require skin grafting."

It was a terrible time to be alone in the city without a family member to turn to for comfort. On the drive home, I felt hollow inside like all there was to me was a shell. It was as if I had no one. The apartment was like a public foyer without any personal warmth. And through it all a pervert started stalking me on the phone.

I had met him at an art gallery bar called Maloney's. He told me that he loved horseback riding and invited me for a Sunday morning ride at Circle M. He never called about the ride, but soon I started getting annoying calls from him at late hours. I begged him to stop, but he persisted. With Robert in the hospital, I dared not ignore the phone ringing. The calls terrified me until I finally had a male neighbor answer the phone a few times. After a few weeks, the calls finally stopped.

I visited with Robert every evening after work and all day Saturday and Sunday, lunching in the hospital cafeteria. We both knew it was going to be a long stretch, and Robert had the hardest part to face. Notwithstanding the excruciating pain from the daily baths and gauze replacements, burn victims are confined to their sterile rooms. He did have a roommate, however, and they were able to play together.

While seeing mom every day may have lifted Robert's spirits, I knew the expectation of a little gift each time would bring an added spark. Fortunately, Dinky cars were the rage, and it brought me great joy to see his face as I gave him a new toy on every visit. The boxes were removed because everything brought into the room had to go through the sterilization chamber. The cardboard would have sizzled. No matter. It was a hit, and the spirit of it all brought me much comfort. Over two months later, Robert had an unrivaled Dinky car collection. I got my son back home, and my spirit's fire was rekindled.

One Friday afternoon, I decided I would pick up Robert, pack the car, call Mom, and head to Ottawa for a loving family weekend.

It was just what we needed after Robert's long confinement. By this time my brother had married Barbara Buchanan, and they had a son named Brian. I knew it would be good for Robert to visit with his cousin. All fired up and ready to go, I called Mom. There are rare times when the stars are not aligned.

"This weekend?" she said. "You mean tonight?"

I felt uneasy. "Why? Don't you want me to come?"

Mom worked as a sales lady Tuesday to Saturday.

"I have to work tomorrow, and I have the flu. I'm so tired. I just don't think this is a good time. What about next week?"

I started to cry. The car was all packed. My fantasies saw me rolling into Ottawa by nine that night. I told my friends I'd be away. I sat home alone all weekend and finally unpacked the car on Sunday. Robert was busy with play, but he witnessed his sad Mommy.

Finally on Sunday night I called my Finnish friend Else Kesonen.

"How was your trip?" she asked.

I started to cry and told her what happened. She burst out laughing. I was stunned.

"Why are you laughing?"

Continuing to laugh, she said, "Look at it this way. You've had a rough summer. You don't have a boyfriend. You had a telephone stalker harass you. You're short on cash. You hate your job, and *now* even your own mother doesn't want you. Don't you see the humor in that?" She laughed uproariously.

I started to laugh and we laughed together. She stretched it further, saying, "When your whole world is collapsing and even your own mother doesn't want you, you just have to laugh." And we kept laughing while I forgave mom for having the flu.

It wasn't that we didn't see Mom often. In fact, since arriving in Toronto, I drove to Ottawa exactly every thirteenth week. That was the week I received an extra paycheck. I needed time with my family. So rain or snow, we made it home. One Christmas morning, the first year I owned my MG Midget, we drove through a terrible, heavy, wet snow storm. For a jaunty, sporty look to match my new car, I wore a fabulous thick, red wool, ski sweater instead of an overcoat. The car was cold. I turned the heat to high. Only a trickle of heat came out of the windshield vent. It was not enough to melt the snow. Even with the wipers dashing furiously from side to side, the windows weren't clear. Every twenty miles or so, I had to pull over and get out of the car and clear the snow away. It was at these times that the snow began to hug my sweater. As it got wetter and heavier, the thought of turning back went through my mind. But all I had to do for motivation was look at the two spirited brown eyes of the little boy sitting beside me on his way to see grandma for Christmas. There was no turning back, and the usual five-hour trip took eight long, laboring hours in the cold.

That spring Robert and I headed up north to visit friends, and I opted to take all the kids for a ride. The kids ran through the mud to get to my car and effortlessly plunked their muddy boots all over the interior. Ah well, it was a sunny day. When the ride was over, I gathered cleaning supplies and crawled in to scrub. As I moved my cloth along the foot well on the passenger side, I saw a flap. I lifted it up. I put it down. I hesitated. I lifted it up. I felt the driver's side. Another flap. I lifted it up. Must be, I thought. I turned on the ignition. I turned on the heat switch. Heat came blasting through the open vents. No more cold winter rides. Well, at least this time I had put in oil and water.

My good reputation still flourished at Mosport Park when news got out I was looking around for a new job. A Montreal couple, Doc Fineberg and his wife had recently bought the track, and they sought me out to be their office manager. Whew! I was back in the fast lane. This time I was going to make sure I stayed there.

Doc was a dentist from Montreal, Quebec. He was eccentric and colorful. He instituted the Executive Pass which was the ultimate card to be wearing at the track. The pass would get one through any doorway, into the executive pits, and into the tower. Only 30 or 40 of these passes were issued, and I always had one. We were running races to crowds of 80,000 to 100,000, and the sport was turning into really big business.

Mosport Park is a forty-five minute drive out of Toronto. One weekend I set up at the Flying Dutchman Hotel a mile or so from the track to give passes to all the drivers and crew as they arrived. The value of the passes was around $25,000.00 and each pass was in an envelope with the driver's names on it.

The hotel was quiet as I finished my preparations at 4:00 a.m., and I asked the bellhop to keep an eye on the box of tickets while I picked up a coffee twenty feet down the corridor.

When I returned minutes later, the box full of tickets was gone. Doc appeared.

"Are all the passes ready, Colleen?" he said with raised eyebrows.

I was startled and couldn't hammer out a response.

Doc pulled out the box and gave me stern warning about my responsibilities. I liked his style. It had POW! The accountant, Harvey Houdas found out and gave me some lip later that day.

Now Doc had a presence and anyone within ten feet of him got to know that he owned Mosport Park. He was a bigger than life kind of man and in the still of the night he asserted his authority over the night clerk. He helped himself to $90,000.00 worth of cash that had been placed in the Flying Dutchman Hotel's safety deposit box by the accountant. When Harvey came down in the morning, he found the box empty. Doc sure had a way with teaching. Eventually though, Harvey bought the track.

While I loved working at Mosport and especially that my son could be with me at the race track, there were still a lot of lonely hours for a single mom. I decided to try my hand at singing again. So, I ordered a Gibson guitar from the Chicago based company. They had a six month waiting list. On the arrival of the guitar, I started a home study course, and soon I was writing and singing my own material. But I needed an audience. I had a plan. I would throw a party serving wonderful food and drinks until midnight. Then out came my stool from behind the bar to the center of the room where I would sit and play and sing. To my surprise, most people stayed to listen. My audience was always comprised of interesting people as I organized "Meet Me" parties. I selected a few single people and asked each to invite a few interesting people. I also asked for any idiosyncrasies about them. My car dealer pal Barry was a talented artist and would sketch their idiosyncrasies on the front of an invitation. No one could resist. Even if they didn't know me, they were curious about how I knew them.

"You'll have to come to the party to find out," I'd tell them.

It was at one of those parties that I met and later dated Herb Capozzie, then owner of the B.C. Lions football team. For a short time, I partied with the social elite and had limousines pulling up to take me to football games. The affluence was nice, but I had an artist's soul and the cocktail crowd failed to inspire me.

Family Day at the Tyson Ranch was more my style, and I gladly accepted a date from Alan MacRae to take Robert and me to this event. Ian and Sylvia Tyson were a folk singing sensation of the 60's and always projected that down home image. Their ranch was just outside of Toronto. The day's activities included a show of roping, hanging with farm animals, and a bar-b-que. At the end of the day with the sun setting, we all gathered in the farmhouse for a sing-a-long.

To my surprise and excitement singer/songwriter Gordon Lightfoot was there. Three weeks earlier, I had paid top price for front row seats at his concert. Now he was five feet in front of me as I sat cross-legged on the floor with the other 40 or so guests. It was magical. Gordon picked up his guitar at Sylvia's insistence and sang at least six songs for us. Ian and Sylvia followed, and then we all sang. I was in a sing-a-long with Lightfoot and Ian and Sylvia. Scrap the limos.

Around that time, another Canadian folk singing sensation was marking the scene. The early days of the now famous Mariposa Folk Festival took place in Orillia, a small town outside of Toronto. My friend David Robins was helping at the front gate and invited me to tag along. While he worked, I was placed in the VIP trailer with the one and only Joni Mitchell. She was there for her first performance at Mariposa. About six of us sat around and talked music business. Joni was a lively participant, always speaking in her signature soft tones. Later she gave an incredible outdoor performance to a packed audience sitting on the grass. With waves of marijuana weaving through the night air, a gentle breeze rippled through Joni's long flowing skirt while her long blonde hair tossed gently in the wind. Her songs were magical, and I sensed everyone there knew they were in the presence of a great talent. That night my love of lyric writing and music blossomed.

****

Penned Moments Remembered

Before his fingers touched the strings
I knew the sounds of his guitar
And though the night had fallen deep
I knew I could not yield to sleep
Until I heard, at least, a single bar.

"Wheelspin" 1963 *Track and Traffic* column by Andre Coffman, containing my first track poem

Have you ever thought how you would feel
With your foot to the floor, hands on the wheel
Speeding around the Mosport track
With not a second to turn and look back
And as you sped your eyes caught sight
And you saw with shock-startled fright
Just as you came down the Andretti straight
Your brother's car spun off at corner eight?
Al Unser knows how he felt that day
Until he saw the pit sign - BOBBY OK.

CHAPTER EIGHT
THE WORLD OF FASHION

As I was good with figures, my name was known in the inner circles of chartered accountants, and it was through them that Unicorn Boutiques found me.

Happy with my situation at Mosport, I wasn't looking for a job when the Unicorn made me an offer I couldn't refuse. It was the summer of 1967, and the Unicorn was a new retailing concept created by an exciting American-born fashion designer, Marilyn Brooks with her husband and general manager John Brooks. Their booming retailing success was outpacing internal organization. Operating three stores in Toronto, one in Vancouver, one in San Francisco, and a garment factory, the paperwork was behind. They had no system in place. For me, it was a challenge. It was also a bigger paycheck, an opportunity to work in a feminine environment, and a chance to be in the trendy area of the city.

Mosport didn't give me up easily, tempting me with my own column in *Track and Traffic* magazine to test drive and report on all new vehicles. However, the fantasy of the Unicorn and its boutiques had more allure. I could imagine the bright colored gifts, Mary Jane candies, and the new hot trends. I eventually joined the Unicorn as Administrative Manager and spun myself into mini skirts and a whole new social world.

The times, they were a-changing. The year was 1967, and the Beatles and the Supremes were topping the charts. The Doors broke with "Light My Fire," José Feliciano won a Grammy Award for his version of "Light My Fire," Dylan was hot, Donovan was hot, and the Beach Boys had a hit with "Good Vibrations." Greenwich Village in New York City was the lively, hip artistic and creative center of the U.S., and Yorkville Avenue in Toronto was its counterpart. Art was gigantic. Andy Warhol elevated the Campbell's Soup can to international prominence simply by painting it in huge proportions.

The world of fashion was exploding with new dynamics, new shapes, new styles, and new colors. The birth of boutiques was in its infancy, and the very gifted and very creative person who started the movement in Canada was my new boss Marilyn Brooks.

Meeting Marilyn was one of the best things to happen to me. During my first interview in the Unicorn offices, Marilyn popped in. We were in her third floor office above the main store. It was overflowing with fabric bolts and swatches, sketches and baskets full of colored pencils and markers, all framing a large antique dining table she used as a desk. In her early thirties, Marilyn was a tall woman with flowing long brown hair. She bounced into the room and filled it with her American charm.

"Hi, everybody," she sang out. She made her way to a chair, stopping to shake my hand and say "Hi! I'm Marilyn Brooks." She was wearing a fabulous two-piece version of a banker's suit. It was in yellow pinstripes, mini-skirted, and double breasted up to a cleavage v-neck. She looked stunning.

I was awestruck. The conservative meeting turned into ringing phones with staff members popping in with new dress samples. Yanka, who became one of Canada's top models, arrived to show Marilyn her portfolio. Everything had a buzz to it. This was all so much prettier than cars. How could I refuse?

I adapted quickly. My business look of camel suits with mid-calf length skirts and white blouses were soon tossed out for multi-colored banlon mini dresses a la Emilio Pucci and clunker high heel shoes. Pex panty hose, the revolutionary all-in-one hose that replaced stockings and garters, were just out, and the Unicorn had them. Designers Mary Quant and Laura Ashley were breaking big in England, and the Unicorn imported their designs. Marilyn was turning out her own new designs daily and the prototypes hit the stores in waves.

Everything about the Unicorn operation was in good taste. As a new way of merchandising fashion, the store was filled with hand painted daisies, hundreds of bunches of dried star flowers, pampas grass, bright colored plumes, and peacock feathers set in straw baskets or clay urns. Paper fish hung from the ceiling, and an array of bold, thick wine goblets (coined Passionella Goblets for Marilyn's friends with a club of the same name) filled the shelves along with brightly colored Peter Max giftware. Marilyn shopped everywhere to find unique gift items. To keep the mystique, the staff was ordered to cut up all shipping labels before putting the packaging in the garbage. She didn't want the competition finding her sources and discovering her secrets. The stores burned incense, and the staff wore trendy new mini dresses obtained through generous discount and weekly bonuses for high sales.

The stores were all in prime locations. As Administrative Manager, I was in charge of the financial flow for the entire operation in Canada and the U.S. Policy changes were necessary to get the finances into shape. As the enforcer, I was not popular with the staff.

"Our sales are down because Colleen moved the cash register." Or, "Our sales are down because Colleen insists on three forms of identification when customers write a check," were a couple of comments. I was the scapegoat for everything. But in time, the accounting took shape. Sales went up. Bad checks were cut by 80%, and I gained respect.

The Cumberland store was situated in a quaint old house with an apartment upstairs. Robert and I moved in a few months after I started working at Unicorn. Living in the hub of activity was a challenge, particularly for child rearing. Not only was the store busy, but Yorkville was filled with drugged-out hippies armed with paint brushes and flowers. During the first week, Robert rushed up the stairs to his third floor room and rushed back down with his piggy bank. A few minutes later, he rushed back up with the bank emptied.

"Mom" he said out of breath with big innocent eyes. "There's this girl, and her mom and dad don't like her, and I gave her all my money so she could eat. I told her she can come in and have a bath. Can she, Mom?" Astonished, I told him no and not to invite anyone else from the street to our home. A new era had begun.

With Robert's ninth birthday coming up in early May, I aimed to adjust the festivities to something more manageable than the previous year and its commitments. On his eighth birthday, I let him invite seven friends to the circus. This was a mistake. Getting eight, eight-year-olds on to streetcars and then seated at the huge circus was a nightmare.

As soon as we were all seated, the kid with the squeaky voice cried out, "Mrs. Riley. I have to go to the bathroom."

I couldn't let him go alone. I couldn't go with him and leave the other kids alone.

"Everybody up and out to the washroom." I said. We squished through the crowds, halting every fifty feet or so to do a head count. Seated again, the wails continued.

"Mrs. Riley. I want a coke," one of them said.

"But the coke man is way down there," I replied.

"Mrs. Riley. I want some popcorn," another piped up.

"But the popcorn man isn't in our aisle anymore," I said.

"You should have got some when I asked you before."

"I want some now," he said with his teeth clenched.

As the memories of the difficulties sprung up, I remembered the worst part. At the end of the day, I told my son he could invite eight kids the next year. Getting out of this wasn't going to be easy, but I was determined at any cost. It cost to extricate myself from honoring the commitment and still be a swell mom.

"Robert," I cooed to him one evening. "For your birthday this year I want you to have a choice. You can invite your eight friends as I promised or you can be King for a Day."

"What do you mean, King for a Day?" he asked.

"Well, as King for a Day," so began the bribe, "you can plan a whole day doing what you want. You can pick the restaurant where we will have brunch. You can plan whatever you want to do in the afternoon, like going to a movie, going sailing, or going for a helicopter ride over Centre Island. And then you can pick the restaurant where you would like to have your birthday dinner."

"Yeah," he said. "But I promised Chris he could come to the circus with me this year."

"Oh, that's not a problem," I said. "Chris and even a couple more of your friends can join us for dinner in the restaurant. We'll have a big birthday cake there too."

"I don't know," he said. "I had fun last year."

"And," I went on, "you get a new outfit for your special day. I'll take you shopping ahead of time and buy you whatever you want."

"But what about presents?" he wailed. "With eight kids I would get lots of presents."

"Here's the special part," I said. "I will buy you whatever really big present you want."

"Okay," he finally said. "I'll call Chris and invite him to dinner. When can we go shopping?"

We had a lot of fun times on these special days, but I do believe the biggest joy for Robert was ordering dinner and then stating to the waiter, "and I don't want any vegetables on my plate."

With the many new friends Robert made at Jesse Ketchum Public School, I started a Friday night "Fright Night" sleepover for the kids. They were invited to bring their sleeping bags, and usually five or six kids joined in to watch the late night fright films on television. I had treats, hot dogs, cokes, and popcorn on hand. But the real winner was the fluffer-nutter breakfast.

After a long late night in which the kids roamed around with flashlights and made silly noises until at least two in the morning, there was one little kid I used to call the "rocket scientist." He would be knocking on my bedroom door at 7:00 a.m.

"Mrs. Riley," he said. "When are you getting up to make our fluffer-nutters?" This special treat was made with toast, peanut butter and marshmallow fluff.

"Later. Later," I answered. "I'll make them later."

Knock, knock. "But I'm hungry now, Mrs. Riley," he went on.

"Can you please get up and make them now?"

I was back at the circus. But whether it was Robert's activities or mine, there was always something going on. Perhaps a bit crazy.

Perhaps a bit different. But always fun. The next adventure was no exception.

Part of the ongoing promotion for the Unicorn was an exciting annual fashion show as only Marilyn could stage. Her shows were unlike the other fashion shows of the time. The others consisted of tea on the eighth floor of Simpson's department store while models gently paraded the runways. Even the annual Judy Awards had older crowds in neck-high brocade gowns with matching coats. This was at a time when mini dresses were exploding everywhere and bare breasts were teasing behind see-through nylon blouses.

"Colleen," Marilyn called in her sweetest voice. "I need you to do something for me."

"I think I'm going to be too busy." I cooed back, knowing I was about to be conned.

"I need you to go to the Judy Awards for me. John and I have to go to an event at the Art Gallery the night of the awards."

"Can I bring a date?"

"Make sure he loves fashion because I'm going to outfit you in something special."

It was a two-piece ensemble with a short sleeves and a tunic top in hugging pink jersey trimmed in olive green. The v-neck plunged to the waist, and it was to be worn braless with matching pants. Yes, "something special."

As Marilyn did the fitting, she murmured, "We're not up for an award this year, but we need to keep our name up front. This will surely get us a picture in the paper. It's all in the line of duty."

The night came and bravely I donned the pink ensemble. Booking agent Lenny Alexander was my date. He didn't know which way to turn when, while helping me on with my coat, my right breast slipped out.

"Oh, my," I thought. "This is going to be some night." And it was. Waiters circled the table all evening while I sat upright, afraid to bend even slightly to sip my soup. Any movement toward the bowl pulled my cleavage forward. Dear old ladies at my table in their high neck pastel, brocade dresses with their husbands who sat at my table peeked breathlessly and quickly diverted their eyes. That was when I forgot what I was wearing and moved my body forward to sip some soup.

Of course Marilyn was right, and I made the newspapers with a photograph larger than any of the Judy Award winners.

In 1969, Marilyn created a fashion extravaganza in Canadian fashion history. A former house model, who was now one of the top five models in the world, Samantha Jones, agreed to be the poster girl.

Nudity was entering the scene. Marilyn envisioned a photo with a girl in a chain bikini with mounds of flowing hair as the poster art we would use to promote her new show. Marilyn's friend, professional photographer Beverly Rockett, agreed to do the shoot, and the show was on. Marilyn booked the O'Keefe Centre with a seating capacity of 3,200. The previous venues sat about 400 people.

It was a big step. But we aimed for a packed house, and we put the tickets on sale at $2.00 each. We sold out in two weeks, in no small way a tribute to the incredible chain bra poster. We even sent an invitation to the Honorable Pierre Elliott Trudeau, Prime Minister of Canada with an enclosed a copy of the poster. We held a row of seats open for him. He declined, but not without mentioning what a stir the poster had caused in the offices of Parliament Hill.

Scheduled on the heels of the spring gardening show, we arranged for the florists to leave their floral garden stage intact, giving us a beautiful setting. At warm-up, the stage was filled with children belonging to staff members parading through the garden. For this event, Marilyn put Robert into a lilac herringbone suit with hipster bell bottom pants. Ah, show business. What did we know; we were from Ottawa.

Absolutely one of the most spectacular show openings ever was when Samantha Jones, with mounds of flowing long blonde hair, wearing a chain brassiere and a pair of white pearlized leather hipster pants, rode a motorcycle down the center aisle of the O'Keefe Centre. POW! Bring on the fashions.

Following such a grand event, Marilyn - the fashion visionary - saw the look for the 1970s as the return of cover-up clothes. To exemplify the point, Marilyn created another explosive poster using the model now actress, Cathy Sheriff, a tall, striking brunette. Cathy was fully dressed in a long black gown and standing in front, tall and dignified, symbolically turning her back on nudity. Behind her was a Roman orgy of nude bodies lying among pedestals eating bunches of grapes. The poster became the talk of the town with all eyes focused on the nudes. Rafael Markowitz, then a television producer who preferred to be addressed as Rif, was contracted to produce the spectacular fashion show named Coliseum '70. It was the largest fashion show produced in Canada to date. The event was staged in the agriculture building at the Canadian National Exhibition with a seating capacity of 8,000 - a number we knew we couldn't reach, but we aimed to take it as high as we could.

The setting was a salute to Roman times complete with Julius Caesar, played by fashion designer David Smith who roared around the big arena in a horse-drawn chariot. Following Caesar were elephants and a parade of Romans. All staff were dressed in togas and bunches of grapes were handed out at the front door. It was a night for dash and fun. Hundreds of drag queens attended in high glamour outfits, easily blending in with the fashion aficionados.

The huge stage had four on-ramps. Center stage was decorated with a Persian carpet on which sat the host, Marilyn Brooks, a live leopard named Pat, and my son Robert donned in a toga. Four giant screens ran live coverage of the fashion parade. - the first use of multi-media at a fashion event. Nearly 4,500 people showed up.

Unknown to the public, high above the crowd, were several sharpshooters ready to take aim in the event the high-volume, high-energy show with its rhythmic drums might bring out the call of the wild in the live animals. Or so Rif told me. This, however, would be the last of the really big shows. But the fun didn't stop there.

CHAPTER NINE
AND THE BEAT GOES ON

Walking into my life during this period of time was a guy named Richard Taunzen. He was a friend of Big Al's, the owner of Al's Service Station on Avenue Road for whom I did part time bookkeeping. What a joy Richard was. We became instant buddies. He had a slight build, wasn't too tall, had light brown hair, was impeccably groomed, and wore tailored suits. He walked into a room with just a hint of arrogance and his shoes as polished as the gleam in his eyes. Bouncing with energy, he was a dream follower. When war broke out in Viet Nam, Richard told me he was heading over there to cash in on the war surplus. When Russia was looking to export bicycles to Canada, Richard had all their brochures and was gung-ho to be an exporter. He wanted me to help him with the details. And then there was the minesweeper, a huge vessel with nets for clearing underwater minefields. He bought it from the Canadian government for only $10,000.00 (as I recall) and docked it in Miami. He had promised to never lose touch with me in his various ventures, so there came a midnight call from Miami.

"Hi, Colleen. It's Richard. Get your bags packed. You and Robert are coming to live in Miami. I've checked the flights and you can be here by 9:00 a.m. tomorrow morning." A big smile crossed my face at the naiveté of the proposal. "Yes, Colleen. You and Robert can come and live on the boat." The big old rusty mine sweeper. "You can be my secretary and have a great new life working on the boat. The weather is fantastic, and I'm in negotiations to lease the boat for the filming of the raising of the Adrea Doria. You can be part of that."

"Besides," he went on, adding what he thought would be the kicker. "It's very hip down here. Jimmy Hendrix (the incredible but drugged out musician) is my neighbor." I could only laugh, but I loved the phone calls.

Richard called again from Miami. His boat was confiscated when he unknowingly took on a cargo of girlie magazines for a client who said it was oranges or something. In any case, until the courts ruled on the disposition of the magazines, he was dry-docked. Guards were on board for the duration. I never heard the end of the story, or if his boat made an entrance into the film world.

The next time I heard from Richard he was in New York heading off to sail to Europe with Lady Sarah Churchill. He had spent time in New York, he told me, cultivating new friends. For this he hired two people: one, a fashion advisor so that he was wardrobed with the current labels, and the other, a public relations person specializing in social situations. With all his charm, he fit in perfectly and was having a wonderful time. He told me he was having discussions with Lady Churchill about opening a string of boutiques in several major cities. He said he would get back to me about it. And he did. Prior to his arrival back in Toronto, he called from Greece to ask me to prepare a financial proposal to open boutiques in Toronto, New York, London and Paris.

I had difficulty feeling serious about my getting involved with Lady Sarah Churchill, but I put the financial package together albeit with sketchy information. Remembering that if I had moved to Miami, Robert and I would have been dry-docked with a cargo of pornography, I couldn't resist a bit of whimsy. Instead of typing a formal presentation, I hand wrote the eight or ten page proposal on pastel colored sheets. This brought no gleam of joy to Richard's eyes. He took it anyway, saying he would use a secretarial service to get it properly set up.

I never heard from or saw Richard again, but I did miss him.

Another proposal of sorts popped into my life not long after I last heard from Richard. One of the "high" places in Toronto was a government-sponsored student residential project named Rochdale. It was an eighteen-storey student co-op near the University of Toronto. The self-governing apartment complex, which opened in September 1968, became a main center to buy and sell drugs. Conveniently, it opened while the police were evicting hoards of drugged-out squatters from nearby Yorkville Village. This group simply shifted locations and headed over to Rochdale.

The students could do whatever they liked in the experimental project, and they decided to keep capitalists out of the retail and office sections of the building. The very nature of their anti-capitalist operations allowed my friends and me to open a recording studio in a small room off the entrance to the indoor parking lot. Just as cars entered the parking area, there was a big sign on the wall "Sound Horn." We became Sound Horn Studios. The project started with David Bleakney and Jim McConnell who were managers of the Downchild Blues Band. They wanted to produce a record album. David asked me to come in as a third partner to help raise money. It was an "arty project" with no chance of making money, but I liked helping people. All I had to do was raise money, and I did. I raised $1,100.00 from Canada's licensing organization. It was $9,000.00 less than we needed. We had no money. We would never make money. We were ideal tenants for the Rochdale board,who gave us free rental space.

The guys found enough burlap at $0.15 a yard to cover the walls and scavenged everywhere for bits and pieces of equipment to buy or borrow. With the sheer will and effort from all the musicians, singers, producers, and friends, Downchild recorded their first album with Sound Horn Studios.

Not long after our success, Rochdale fell apart. The decaying interior was rife with stinky mattresses, holes in walls, broken down doors and garbage-laced corridors. Its journey was over. The neighbors cheered. The taxpayers gave a sigh of relief. I never entered the doors of Rochdale. I was always terrified that the 24-hour surveillance cameras would capture my entrance and Mounties would show up at my door to drill me about drug dealings. But I was proud to be part of the album.

The Unicorn was going through twists and turns before its eventual collapse in 1972. Marilyn and John Brooks had separated, leaving the business to John. Trying to run a business and stage a divorce at the same was not possible. Marilyn and I left the business in 1971 and faced the unemployment line.

The *Ottawa Journal* newspaper once profiled my fun, "mod" apartment. Now I was facing a bundle of debts and a son to raise while on unemployment. I felt the squeeze. I decided it was time to start my own business. I opted for freelancing so I could work from home and spend more time with my son. My debtors received a personal note asking them to hold off for six months. Most of them complied.

Without knowing what services I would offer, I simply made myself available for hire. For an hour, for a day, for a week - but not permanently - I was available for any creative task. I called on the business people I knew and stated, "You've worked with me on various projects. You probably know better than I what I'm capable of, so if you need my help part time, give me a call."

Within the first hour Rafael Markowitz called.

"Colleen," he said. "Come over to my place. I want you to be my press agent."

"But I hardly know anything about press work," I replied.

"You can do it. What you don't know, I'll teach you." Rafael lived a block away in the small, quaint Windsor Arms Hotel. It boasted one of the finest restaurants in the world, Three Small

Rooms. Later, the hotel added the Courtyard Café, a huge sunfilled restaurant which quickly became Toronto's hottest spot. Markowitz was producing television shows like *Party Game* and working mostly in Hamilton some 45 minutes away. It made sense for him to have a full time chauffeur and a stretch Cadillac limousine housing TV monitors in the back seat. He always worked in style.

Except for his black Cadillac, Rafael Markowitz (or Rif), was in his "white" phase. He dressed in white: white shoes, white suits, white coats, white scarves, and white gloves. He never relented. He conducted business meetings from a small two room suite. His secretary occupied the anteroom. His office was stark white. Surrounded by plush white carpeting, a throne was built dead center in the middle of the room. Atop the throne was a white leather swivel chair. On either side of the chair was a Lucite table. One contained a telephone and the other an appointment book. That was it. There was no place for visitors to sit. If one wanted to get near him one had to mount the steps to the throne.

I wasn't intimidated. It was all show business.

Later, in his black silk period, he took a larger suite and furnished it with a wonderful large mahogany desk, a big comfy chair, and most important, a small alarm clock on his desk. For visitors he provided a small, uncomfortable, antique sofa, placed some distance from his desk. Always plagued by salespeople, entrepreneurs, and dreamers, he did give them an opportunity to present their pitch.

"I'm a busy man," he would state as he picked up his clock and set the alarm, "so you have fifteen minutes."

When he went out to see a new band at the Coq d'Or on Yonge Street, his chauffeur would call first to make a reservation.

"Please," he would say. "Mr. Markowitz just wants a quiet corner and don't alert anyone that he's coming."

Who was he? Not many people knew, but after a call like that the room would buzz. On arrival the chauffeur entered the club first, announced the arrival, and checked out the room and the reserved table before Rif made his entrance. A tall, handsome and slight man, Rif would stride in, outfitted in the finest black suit, silk stockings, and Italian leather shoes. He would be seated and his muscle-bound chauffeur would stand behind him with his arms crossed. The irony was that he really was scouting for talent.

Rif hired me to get his name in the paper three times a week and to make sure he was never referred to as "Randy Dandy the Clown," a throwback to his early years. He also wanted the word "producer" before or after his name. We began cranking out fun stories that the media loved, and within three months some entertainment editors gave me home numbers to use until midnight for any late breaking stories.

When Katherine Hepburn was doing *Coco* at the O'Keefe Center and staying at the Windsor Arms Hotel, her limousine accidentally bumped into Rif's limo in front of the hotel. I called a *Toronto Star* columnist, and the next morning the headline in "Around Town with

Jeremy Brown" read "Hepburn makes hit with Caddy." The story included Producer Markowitz. A simple story, but it kept his name in the paper.

Nicole Morin, a stunning French-Canadian actress, knocked the socks off Toronto audiences when she appeared nude in the stage production of *Spring Thaw* in 1970. While nudity was a popular movement at the time, it was the perfection of her body that had the crowds gasping. In blue lighting, the 5' 8" statuesque blonde had the whole city talking. Rif was first on the block with a management contract. She signed, and I became her press agent too. She starred in early Canadian films like the award winning *Goin' Down the Road*, directed by Don Shebib and a film by Ivan Reitman, *Foxy Lady*. She became a regular on the *Party Game* television game show.

With her Parisian-influenced, French-Canadian accent, she was charming, and we hit it off right away. The basic promotion was similar to Rafael's - keep her name alive even if there wasn't an event to hang it on. This gave me a lot of leeway, and basic instinct showed me how. Nicole and I would attend a major event like a charity night attracting crowds of 2,000 to 3,000 people.

On arrival, I told Nicole, "Have faith, and follow me." Forward I strode, my arms gesticulating while I announced in a clear authoritative voice, "Clear the way. Nicole Morin is arriving."

The people would turn and look and move aside, creating a star-like path, and Nicole would follow. She was so breathtaking that everyone was in awe. Most Canadians did not know who Nicole was unless they were in show business. The Canadian movie industry was not high profile, and there was no star system. An actor had to make it in America to be recognized. That is not to say we were without celebrities. People with flair like Garth Drabinsky, founder of Cineplex Theaters, were always in the news. The challenge with Nicole was to get her the recognition she deserved as if we *did* have a star system.

The media surrounded Nicole anytime she made a public appearance. When the first Ontario lottery took place one summer on a boat on Lake Ontario, the organizers called to ask Nicole to draw the first ticket. It had some promotional merit, but the event itself might upstage her. Giving her the star treatment, I insisted that her biography and her photos be included with the press material and that she be highlighted in their press release. They agreed, reminding me that the big story was really the lottery launch.

The next morning there was a big picture story about Nicole, mentioning somewhere that she had drawn the first lottery ticket.

She was a press agent's dream.

Most men who met Nicole were immediately drawn to her, and in big events there could easily be fifty men trying to date her. This could create a dicey situation. Once, two of them were sponsors from Players Cigarettes, when Nicole was Miss Players 1973. They expected a little more. The contracts never specified dinner with clients, but some men soured when they were turned down. So, I carried a stack of business cards while Nicole smiled her way through the room saying how delightful dinner would be. Then she'd turn, point, and say, "That's my manager over there. Just make the arrangements with her. I'm not sure of my schedule."

I'd hand out my card with my number on it, but rarely did anyone call. I suspect the next night when they were home with their wives, they didn't think it would be such a good idea.

One of the funnier times was getting the Eatons men mixed up in the preparation for a charity gambling night Nicole was headlining. It was a big event, and a gambling school agreed to let the organizers shoot pre-publicity shots in their facility. We organized a fabulous casino style costume from the CBC wardrobe department with black net stockings, a black satin bustier, and a fabulous striking pink feather boa. With this, Nicole wore three inch spike heels, making her 5' 11" tall.

Earlier Nicole had been to a party where she met the four Eaton brothers from the T. Eaton Department Store chain, one of the oldest and largest chains in Canada. One of them caught her eye, and she asked me to help her meet him even though she couldn't remember his name. I consulted with a knowledgeable friend, providing her with Nicole's description. George Eaton, it was concluded, was the guy. At the time, he had stepped away from the family retailing empire and was promoting rock concerts.

I suggested to Nicole that an opportune time for her to meet George might be to ask him to attend the charity function as her escort. She loved the idea.

Although I didn't recall seeing any member of the Eaton family ever publicly endorsing a particular charity, I still made the call to Eaton's lawyer. I extended the invitation that George chaperone Nicole for the event and also attend the pre-publicity press conference. A few days later the lawyer confirmed George would love to go. Wow!

The morning of the press conference, Nicole was at the CBC getting dressed and coiffed. I arrived early at the gambling school to meet the press and George Eaton. He was a bit shy, but I went over the staging of the morning's activities and tried to put him at ease.

Nicole arrived late and in a flurry with feather boas flying everywhere. She headed straight to the washroom, and I followed. The two of us burst out laughing.

"Is he here?" she asked. "I'm so nervous. Do I look all right? My God, Colleen, what are we doing?" And we just kept laughing.

I pushed the door open, winked at Nicole, and proudly announced her arrival to the twenty or so press photographers, cameramen and writers. Within seconds the light bulbs were flashing, and she was proudly posing and flouncing her boas.

"Let's get some shots by the teller's cage," I called out.

I directed the cameras and crew to the teller's cage and took Nicole over to meet George Eaton. Introductions made, Nicole looked over his face and said in her charming French accent,

"Oh, you've shaved off your beard?"

George's hand reached up to his face where he felt his cheek and said,

"No. No I didn't. I never had a beard."

"Oh," she said, "I thought you did."

"Yikes! He is the wrong Eaton," I thought.

Keeping the show on the road, I went right into my promotional smile, introduced George to the media and staged some publicity shots around the prominent brass cage. The three of us went to lunch at Three Small Rooms. I left early in case there was an opportunity for the wrong match up to evolve into something. However, it did not happen, and Eaton's lawyer called shortly thereafter to advise me that George would not be attending Casino Night with Nicole. In the meantime, the *Toronto Star* newspaper printed a smashing picture with Nicole and George which was a great benefit to the charity.

Quickly, Rafael Markowitz was climbing the ladder of production circles, and he landed one of CHCH TV's biggest productions, the *Hilarious House of Frightenstein*. The children's series drew the likes of Vincent Price, Shelly Berman, and other stars. As it was a big production, he moved to a thirteen room mansion on Royal York Road complete with an indoor split-level rock garden and a kidney-shaped swimming pool. It was so Hollywood.

My other assignments included picking up stars with the limousine and having access to the "briefcase telephone," a rare novelty at the time. The fun was to make a phone call just a few steps outside

THE LIFE AND TIMES OF A SINGLE WOMAN

the doorway of the person you were meeting to say you'd be there any minute. Seconds after the call, you'd knock on their door. The reactions were amazing when you showed them the telephone in the briefcase. This new technology was just beginning.

On one assignment, Vincent Price was arriving for a four day shoot and eight media interviews. We discovered he loved black jelly beans. This was not an item readily available so Rafael sent at least five of his staff to buy all the jelly bean bags they could find and separate out the black ones. Everything went smoothly. For the interviews, I sat Mr. Price poolside by a waterfall backdrop with a crystal bowl of jelly beans on the side table. It was a big event for the Toronto show business industry, and we accomplished our goal of making Vincent Price feel comfortable. Rafael was nowhere to be seen when the press were around.

He was never visible to the media. I handled all the printed material, all the telephone calls, and all the interviews. Eventually a mystique was created, and the press were demanding to know the inside stories. Our lips were sealed. All staff members and crew were alerted not to speak. There was a lot of buzz about researchers who were calling any number of people Rafael knew. Finally, a full-page story broke in the *Toronto Star* written by Marcy McDonald. It compared Rafael to Howard Hughes of the Howard Hughes Tool Corporation, the infamous Hollywood tycoon who eventually went into seclusion. Rafael told me he hated the story and declared he never wanted to see his name in print again. He went into seclusion.

My services were terminated on a friendly note. He got exactly what he wanted. He had, I found out later, registered the company name Markowitz Tool Corporation. The more I thought about him, the more the Howard Hughes Tool Corporation and its eccentric owner popped into my mind.

So began my foray into press and publicity work. Marilyn was also freelancing, and we linked up for a few projects. We opened David's Footwear at Bay & Bloor where we put live models in the windows. For Bill Brack's Sports Car Boutique, we staged a fashion show with a hot pink muffler dress, a map light v-neck dresses, and coil springs mounted to Pierre Cardin leather boots.

One Friday night as Marilyn and I sat in her apartment sipping wine while having one of our creative meetings, artist John Gould dropped by with a problem. John had recently returned from a commissioned world tour to sketch mime artist Marcel Marceau. He was now trying his hand at animated film and needed to find an eight-year-old boy with a scruffy voice.

"Will this do?" I scratched out using my *Exorcist* voice.

Three days later, I was in a recording studio doing voiceovers for John's films. While hamming around at the studio, I was given several more parts using various tones and accents. The pay was excellent, and I loved the flexibility. Freelance working presented a new challenge.

CHAPTER TEN
AN AFFAIR WITH A MARRIED MAN

Yorkville Avenue was always buzzing with celebrities in the late 1960's. Besides the coffee house performers who hung out in the area, record promotion teams often brought their big acts to Yorkville to schmooze in one of the exciting restaurants.

A longtime fixture on the street was a nursing home, the original Mount Sinai Hospital. It was a stately old mansion set back from the street about twenty-five feet. An ornate, wrought iron fence wrapped around the front garden where the elderly and infirm would sit on fair weather days. From there, they observed the emerging drug culture taking place right before them.

The front of the wrought iron fence became a favorite lounge spot for spaced out hippies and flower children. Mostly gentle folk, one hippy might generate a low level pitch to sell drugs to a passerby, but overall there was an admiration and respect on both sides. One might say there were good vibrations as these two different groups bridged the generation gap.

Yorkville's main parking lot was also used to park a trailer called 'The Odyssey'. This was a free drop-in, drug treatment center. An active place, it wasn't uncommon to witness someone crawling around the trailer barking like a dog or a young man reciting poetry while wearing fresh daisies behind his ear.

We lived a block south on the more refined Cumberland Street where the old guard still walked their poodles on Sunday afternoons. The street was filled with candle shops and boutiques nestled inside quaint old homes. A tiny basement restaurant that seated about four people was a few doors over. Singer Murray McLauchlan, among other singer/musicians, could often be seen there, chomping down the breakfast special. It was on this street in a two-story apartment above a store that I lived as a single parent with my son Robert.

Because he was in bed by 7:30 p.m., the nights could be lonely. I kept socially active, however, by cooking dinner for four each night and inviting friends to dine with us each evening.

Every month or two I threw a spaghetti bash, usually on a Friday night. Herb Capozzi, the former manager of the B.C. Lions, who I dated earlier, taught me a great recipe. I embellished it and for years worked on making it distinctively mine. It became famous in my small circle of friends, especially after Lou Reed (of the Velvet Underground) sanctioned it. More on that later.

It was in the fall of 1970 that my friend Walt Jamieson of RCA Records called to ask if he could invite José Feliciano and his wife Hilda to a spaghetti bash I was having for about thirty friends.

"José is playing in Yorkville at the Penny Farthing," Walt said. "I thought it would be nice if we strolled over after the show."

"Sure, Walt," I said. "Bring them over."

The party, which was filled with beautiful people draped over each other, was a big success. Marijuana, and who knows what else, was prevalent and not easily outlawed from a home in downtown Yorkville. I, however, was never inclined toward drugs and instead sipped wine and spooned out bowls of spaghetti. The Felicianos and Walt didn't make it, having gotten involved with other friends. But, strangely, this did not preclude my meeting José.

A year later, Marilyn Brooks, invited me to a Saturday night dinner party with José Feliciano. Touring without his wife, José was appearing the next day at the O'Keefe Center. Marilyn was dating Efrem, a percussionist who had drummed with José, and the gathering was scheduled for 10:00 p.m. on Saturday, November 5, 1971.

It was mid-Saturday morning when Marilyn called. Robert, then ten years old, had already left to join his friends for a pajama party that weekend. I had a date planned for later.

"Sorry, Marilyn," I said. "I already have a date for tonight."

"But, Colleen," she said. "This is a date with José Feliciano."

Quite frankly, while I loved his music, rock stars and entertainment people did not impress me as dating material.

"I know, Marilyn, but I just saw him on TV doing *This Is Your Life*, and he has a wife." I defended my position.

"Maybe they've broken up," she enthused. "Trust me, Colleen. I can feel it in my bones. You know that I know every beautiful model in Toronto, but I'm not inviting any one of them because in my heart of hearts I know there's something special about you two."

I was capitulating. "But what about my date?"

"Cancel it," she answered. "José will only be here for two days. You can date the other guy any time. Besides, you may never want to see him again after you meet José."

How could I say no?

Robert had never been away before and having the apartment to myself was a great luxury. I soaked in the tub for a long time . . . with the door open. I manicured my nails, conditioned my hair, shaved my legs, and played with bubbles. All the while I listened to music from José's *10 to 23* album which I had purchased a year earlier. I was beginning to believe in Marilyn's instincts. I thought about the year before. We had almost met. Now, on his first trip back to Toronto, I was again being asked to meet him. Twice he was being introduced into my life. Would there be a third sign?

Born into poverty in Lares, Puerto Rico and blind from birth, José succeeded far beyond the average musician. He rose to the top. I admired his talent.

I had never met a blind person, but I sensed that I should wear a soft fabric, so I chose a full length, gray velvet turtleneck dress with long slits up each side. It was an outfit I had created for myself. As it was a chilly November night, I topped it with a Marilyn Brooks design - a full length, pearlized, lime green leather coat. It was pure vogue.

The old Ward Price Auctioneer's buildings on Carlton Street had a wonderful third floor apartment complete with fireplace and a forty-five foot living room, and this was Marilyn's home. It was beautifully decorated. A grand piano sat next to a concave bar. All were gathered there as I made my entrance. Marilyn beamed with excitement at my presence.

"It's Colleen," she excitedly cheered out with her voice trailing as she turned toward the other end of the room where José was standing. "Colleen is here," she went on almost singing it out.

Introductions made and feeling strangely shy, I sat with a couple of friends in front of the fireplace while José, Efrem, and the others stood around the bar listening to José's new album *That the Spirit Needs*.

The sound of Marilyn's voice rang out once more, "Colleen. I think José is hungry. Could you please bring the tray of hors d'oeuvres?"

I picked up one of the trays and offered the food around. Marilyn grabbed my arm and whispered, "Put that tray down and stay here."

So there I was standing beside José. He was wearing a fragrance. It was Aramis. It was nice.

As the song "Daytime Dreams" began, I touched his hand to let him know who was talking and said, "That's a nice song."

"Oh, do you like it?" he enthused. "I wrote that one with Edward Conley."

"Really," I said, "and what was your inspiration?"

We continued to talk, still touching. We talked and we talked, moving over to the chocolate brown velvet sofa and continuing to talk. At one point I asked, "Are you married?"

José cleared his throat, "I'm on my way to a divorce."

His wife Hilda was still his manager, and they still lived together. But things weren't working, and they were separating. Hey. He was blind. It's not like he could just walk out the door. I took everything at face value.

As we talked through the night, José told me stories of growing up. As a child he didn't know the significance of blindness and acted like all young boys. Sounds were important to him, and he would get into his mom's cupboards to find cans to drum on. His mother would hide the cans, but he would always find them by touch. I was able to share some of my own life stories. Soon we were in deeper territory than I had treaded with any other man.

At an early age he had shot into pop stardom and was filled with boyish glee about everything. I was moving forward in my career and was on my own high. Everything felt right. His thick, shoulder length hair fell over his face as he talked, and I began to glide my fingers through the silky mass, studying his face as I did so. He had wonderful high cheekbones, smooth skin, beautiful teeth, and a great smile. Dawn was upon us, and we decided to head over to José's hotel.

Being with a blind person seemed natural to me. I was able to direct him, inform him, and not walk him into posts. I was comfortable as his guide except when I was tripping on my long, lime green leather coat. I questioned whether I could close my eyes and let someone walk *me* along. The thought frightened me and also heightened my awareness. I learned quickly how to act and react safely with his sweet hand on mine as we made our way through street traffic.

José had a matinee performance on Sunday at the O'Keefe Center a few blocks from the Royal York Hotel where we had spent a glorious night. We strolled over to the theatre, both feeling a little shy and a little moonstruck. But the best was yet to come.

Sitting out front at the concert with Marilyn and Efrem, my heart was racing as we waited for the show to begin. I had never seen José live in concert and didn't know what to expect. He walked on stage with manager Bob Drew at his side. He climbed up on his stool, picked up his guitar, adjusted the mike and said, "Hello Toronto."

The audience cheered. "You know, Toronto has some really good looking Mommas." Applause. "I know because I met one last night, and she's a real cool Momma." Then he broke into song.

My heart was racing. He was talking about me. I listened to his songs intently. I watched his hands fly across the strings of his guitar. His music filled the room; each performance brought thunderous applause. I was excited. I tried to reconcile the performer and the man with whom I spent the night. It was like José had become another person, and I was attracted to both. I almost felt guilty in liking one over the other. It stayed that way for years. On one hand he was my mentor, my friend, and my guy. When he was close to me, I felt complete. On stage he was my sexy rock star, and the excitement of his performances turned me on. He was two lovers; I was mesmerized.

After the show, we headed back to the hotel, and I found myself holding his hand a little bit tighter and feeling a bit closer to him. Marilyn, Efrem, and Paulinho Magalhaes (José's percussionist and best friend) joined us. Hotel management sent a basket of fruit and cheeses to José's room, and we sat around talking.

José and I were seated on the side of the bed, holding hands and still very excited. Neither of us had much sleep, and we were on a nervous high. Then suddenly, as we sat laughing at some silly story, one of José's glass eyes popped out and fell to the floor. I didn't know his eyes had been removed. I froze, and then I leaned down and picked it up.

"I have your eye here in my hand, José," I said.

"Thank you," he said quietly. "Could you just give it to Paulinho so he can rinse it off?"

"Of course," I said.

It was an intimate and sensitive moment, the eye burning into my palm with the impact of a moment with God.

I seized on that moment to absorb the dynamics. The night before I had made an uninformed decision that somewhere in his far depths José could see me. I wanted to believe that a vision of me was registering at a level different than a person with normal eyesight. It wasn't. This physicality didn't upset me, but mentally I struggled for understanding. The deeper I thought, the closer I felt to José. And the closer I got, the more awkward I felt in his presence. Those moments were incredible glimpses that spoke a thousand words. My soul was stilled and this excitement began creating a path to my heart. I wanted into José's world. I wanted to stay there forever.

I regained my composure, surrendering the eye to Paulinho who quickly and quietly rinsed it and returned it to José. He gently returned the eye to its socket. He reached for my hand, and I snuggled over a bit closer.

The afternoon was filled with jokes and funny stories. José loved entertaining and being entertained. Between himself, Paulinho, and Efrem, they had countless on-the-road anecdotes to share. Marilyn, as always, kept the room bubbling.

Around 5:00 p.m., I dashed home to have dinner with Robert, organize a babysitter, and change before returning to José's side in his dressing room backstage at the O'Keefe. We locked hands as we made our way to the side stage.

José leaned over and declared, "You have to come to New York with me in the morning."

I was startled. "I don't know. I can't just leave. I have a son to look after."

"Just say yes." He then turned his head in the direction of Bob Drew, "Hey, Bob, can you arrange to get Colleen on our flight in the morning?"

Bob approached José, "We can talk about that later. Right now you're due on stage."

"But, José," I stammered. "I didn't say I would go with you."

José hugged me, "Then I'm not going on stage until you say yes."

Marilyn eased over and whispered, "Tell him what he wants to hear."

Bob Drew spoke with authority, "José, it's time to get on the stage."

The audience started clapping.

José turned to me, "It's up to you. Are you coming?"

"I promise," I whispered in his ear, "I'll tell you at intermission."

"Okay," he said. "As long as you say yes." With that, he released my hand and walked out to his cheering fans.

For that performance, he told the audience he met a Toronto Momma who couldn't make up her mind, but he was sure she would see things his way. After that, he always included something about me in his shows or slipped my name into his songs when I was in the audience. How could I not go to New York?

It was around 10:00 p.m. that same night when I called and lied to my Uncle Palma. "I just got a call from New York from a very important client. Can you baby-sit Robert for three days?" My wonderful Uncle Palma agreed to stay with Robert. I dashed home after the concert, prepared three days of school lunches and frozen dinners for Robert and my Uncle, packed for New York, and slept for a few hours.

I had never been away with a man before. I had never flown. Both scenarios put me in a state of panic. How could I just be with someone for three days without a notebook in my hand and a promotion to work out? Would we have enough to talk about? What if he was bored with me after one day? What holds an airplane up?

None of the questions needed to be answered once I saw José at the airport the next morning. The flutters in my heart left no room for nagging questions. Bob Drew, who was busy organizing José's 21 pieces of luggage, greeted me warmly. He gave me my ticket and took my overnight bag. We were off.

The trip to New York was to promote José's new album. He was booked for several radio interviews as well as a guest spot with TV talk host, David Frost. We were staying at the Times Square Hotel, a decrepit old building with run down rooms. A bent coat hanger served as a TV antenna. We chuckled as I provided commentary on our surroundings. José slipped out of the room to do a couple of radio interviews and returned about an hour later. He picked up his guitar and while he adjusted the strings, he said, "Colleen, I have to practice now. I practice every day for at least two hours. I hope you don't mind."

I was in awe just to be with him. The sounds of his guitar filled the room. I sat back in a chair and closed my eyes. Blocking out all the visuals for long periods of time was arresting. I could hear better. My thoughts were clearer, and I felt a strong connection to José.

Every once and a while José would ask, "How are you doing? Are you okay?" and then return to practicing. He eventually put down the guitar. As I tried to play it, he pulled me into his arms. I loved the vulnerability. I loved giving myself freely at any hour of the day. I loved the incredible passion of this young, hot blooded Latin. I felt I was all woman, physically and mentally.

Those born under the Virgo sign, I had read, are slow to ignite but when aroused have a white heat greater than all other signs. We discovered we were both Virgos and the stars played a part in the magnetic pull we felt. We also discovered each other's ages – he was 26 and I was 31.

"Oh, Colleena, Colleena. You're the oldest woman I ever dated." He picked up the guitar and from the Rod Stewart song "Maggie May" © broke in at the lines, "The morning sun when it's in your face really shows your age."

In horror, I jumped up and ran to the mirror. I didn't see any wrinkles. Whew! "We're equal then because you're the oldest man I ever dated. This year anyway."

"But the song goes on to say," José came back. "But you turned into a lover and mother what a lover, you wore me out." He reached out for me, took me in his arms, and whispered, "It doesn't matter how old you are. I'm happy being with you. I'm glad you're here."

We took a stroll in Times Square, the triangular center and hub of New York City. There I gave an account of the thousands of people standing on every sidewalk, their clothing styles and how old they were. I read all the neon advertising signs. Arm in arm and hand in hand, we were lost in our dreamy world. We were always in physical contact. We had to be. It was hypnotic and romantic. Our hands expressed what our eyes could not.

As we walked the last strip of the triangle, a figure suddenly darted out about to attack me. He made a grab for my purse. He missed.

"Drop your purse, lady," he said.

José dropped my hand and quickly jumped in front of me.

"Back off!" José shouted.

Startled, the thief froze. An onlooker yelled out, "Hey, José. José Feliciano," and the thief was gone. I threw my arms around José and whispered, "You're my hero."

The next day José had a 2:00 p.m. rehearsal for the David Frost Show and a taping later in the day. Paulinho came by to pick out José's clothing, and the three of us left together. The studio was about five blocks away, and a *Rolling Stone* photographer made arrangements to shoot José strolling the streets of New York. We were soon hit with light bulbs flashing and the sounds of a clicking camera.

José took the photographer aside, "I don't mind you taking pictures, but don't print any with a girl on my arm."

"No problem, man," and he kept on clicking. I never appeared in *Rolling Stone*.

José, Paulinho, and I decided to eat at a cozy spot in Times Square. Sitting in a booth covered in maroon vinyl, I was glad to be in the company of someone who knew José. Paulinho was Portuguese and spoke with a heavy accent. He was always upbeat, always ready with a smile and truly loved and admired José. Paulinho, about fifteen years José's senior, was his mentor. In his early forties, he knew a lot about life and was able to guide José. Both were Latinos, loved women and spoke romantic languages. When Paulinho wanted to address José privately they spoke in Portuguese or Spanish.

"Excuse me, Colleen," Paulinho would start. "I have to talk to the little boy." This phrase was used when he wanted José to see things his way. Then the two of them would talk in Spanish. Over coffee Paulinho told the story of the psychic events that happened when we met in Toronto.

"You see, what happened, Colleen, was a big surprise to me," Paulinho started. "About ten years ago I met a woman in Brazil, and I saw her for a while. Then I moved to Los Angeles, was on the road, and lost her number. In fact, I was so busy I didn't really think about her."

He looked up with his warm round eyes. "You know what I mean. I was on the road all the time. I just lost track. Over the past couple of years I started thinking about her, and I tried to call her. But I couldn't find her number. I made all kinds of inquiries. I contacted old friends, family, information services, but I couldn't find out anything."

He sat up straight and continued.

"You walked into the room. Marilyn was calling out your name, and I looked up. There in front of my eyes like a neon sign in the sky - the phone number for the woman flashed before me. It was a miracle. I looked into your eyes to see who you were, to see if I knew you. I couldn't believe it. It was magic. I told José. And now, here you are in New York with José, and we're having coffee. It must mean something."

I was breathless. I took this as a third sign. Three signs. Yes, he was right. It must mean something.

Paulinho became a trusted friend and was the liaison for José and me. He wrote to me from around the world. He sent me travel schedules and messages from José. He believed I was José's soul mate and promoted our togetherness, yet he never filled me with unrealistic expectations. With pride and dignity, he did what he could to bring us together without causing interference. The affair may never have gone on without that connecting link. Hanging out with a major star means offering a lot of availability, which I didn't have, and living in close proximity, which I didn't. Paulinho kept me in touch, and I kept him in touch. Through it all, José heard the stories I sent from Toronto.

The New York departure came too soon. José filled me with promises of many phone calls and seeing me soon. I invited him to Toronto for Christmas. He told me he had met someone recently named Susan and had agreed to spend Christmas in Detroit with her family. That was disappointing, but it added credence to his declaration of an impending divorce. In the end, I think he stayed at home with his wife in California.

"Oh, well," I thought. "Big rock star. I too had a busy life and fabulous show business promotions coming up. So I had fun, but maybe it was just a weekend fling." I decided to put it on the back burner until I heard from him again. However, everyday life wouldn't let me forget. Stores, offices, and restaurants had just discovered Muzac©, and "Feliz Navidad"© and other Feliciano songs were being played everywhere. Getting José off my mind was not going to be easy. It was thrilling to hear his music while shopping in a busy dress shop. My thoughts shifted to that first moment of excitement.

I remembered sitting on Marilyn's sofa with the morning sun creeping through antique leaded glass windows. I remembered the feeling of José's silky hair against my skin. I remembered, too, his soft caress as he found his way inside the slits on my velvet dress, and how my heart pounded as I waited breathlessly for Jose to pull the word 'yes' from my lips. These memories would not be stilled.

THE LIFE AND TIMES OF A SINGLE WOMAN

It was time to go home. I didn't want to think about him. I just wanted to get ready for Christmas.

Penned Moments Revisited

You complete the orchestration
For the waltz I hear within
But I need you as a conductor
For the dancing to begin

CHAPTER ELEVEN
MY SECOND DATE WITH JOSÉ

When I slid away to New York to be with José, I was surprised that it became fodder for gossip immediately. A few people called Marilyn when they couldn't reach me, and she was so excited that she told them where I was. He was a man. I was a woman. It was a date, and I had no idea of the impact of fame.

To digress for a moment, by the time I met José, he was performing in England, France, Italy, Spain, Australia, New Zealand, Scandinavia, Canada and Latin American. By 1966, he was commanding audiences of over 100,000 people in Central and South America, and his Spanish language records were commanding high volume sales. His success in the USA started in 1968 with his first big hits in the English language "Light My Fire," and "California Dreamin'," and his first gold album *Feliciano*. By 1972, José had recorded in Italian, Spanish, and Portuguese and had earned twenty-nine gold albums around the world.

In the spring of 1969, he was awarded two Grammies by the National Academy of Recording Arts and Sciences. One was for Best New Artist, and the other was for Best Male Contemporary Pop Vocal Performance for "Light My Fire."

José made many guest appearances on network television shows and specials with stars like Bing Crosby, Tom Jones, Glen Campbell,

Andy Williams, and The Carpenters. He also had his own *Feliciano - Very Special* show on NBC. He was a big star.

On my return from New York, I received a call from Rafael.

"How was your trip to New York with José Feliciano?" he asked.

I froze. Up to this point nobody ever cared what I did with my personal life.

"You know about my trip?" I said.

"Doesn't everybody?" he came back.

How many people knew, I wondered? As a teen from the moral fifties, I embraced a reasonable fear of being declared an unfit mother if my behavior was considered inappropriate.

Anxious to hear all the news, Marilyn met me for lunch that day at the trendy Mermaid Restaurant on Bay Street. I arrived in a flap.

"Who did you tell about my trip with José?" I asked.

Marilyn smiled, "Just a few people who called looking for you. But don't worry about it. Just tell me all about New York."

As we started talking, Ann Taylor, a model, came by with a big grin, and leaned into my shoulder saying, "Hi Colleen. How was your weekend with José Feliciano? Great Stuff!"

I looked up and saw she was sitting with three other models, all looking over and grinning. I was blushing and said, "It was wonderful."

I worked with about 200 models, booking them for jobs in stores and shopping plazas. I suspected they all knew or would know. Oh, God. What did you get me into, Marilyn?

We finished lunch laughing, knowing that what was happening was bigger than the gossip that swirled around it. Well, Marilyn knew. She was a visionary. I wasn't so sure I would hear from him again.

With the demise of the Unicorn, I had given up my great downtown apartment. Downtown landlords posted big signs in their front hallways stating "No Children Allowed." We were forced to move out of the inner core and into a high rise building far from downtown. Used to all the excitement of Yorkville, the drop-ins, the dinner parties, life in our new apartment on Marlee Avenue was no fun except for the indoor swimming pool. Having given up my car when we lived downtown, we were also forced to use public transportation. But it was from this new place that I began to build my creative consulting and press business. It was also where I lived when I finally met José.

His records became a way of reconnecting with him and the upbeat life I had enjoyed. José autographed the album he gave me *That the Spirit Needs,* and my hands would brush across his writing as I slipped the LP out. I vacillated between feeling romantic and being practical. Who was he really? He was still married, and he also had a girlfriend in Detroit. Maybe he had other girls in other cities. After all, he had Latin blood. Latinos were known as lovers.

It was a potentially messy situation, and I thought I should get out early. With hardly any time to ponder the situation, the phone rang two weeks later.

"Hi, Colleen. It's José."

"It is. Oh, hi. Oh my goodness. I didn't expect to hear from you so soon," I stammered back with my heart racing.

"I'm coming to Toronto for a few days, and I'd like to see you," he said.

I felt like I was a thermometer dropped into hot water. My face glowed. I was so excited.

"Of course," I said. "I want to see you again. When are you coming? I'll meet you at the airport." I couldn't resist him.

I didn't know if he was married or dating, but he told me he pushed his agent to get him more gigs in Toronto because he wanted to see me. He was so romantic.

José was coming to Toronto to appear as a guest on the television series *Kenny Rogers and the First Edition*, produced by Michael Steele. We agreed to meet at the airport. I arrived two hours ahead of time as a kind of pre-extension to the visit. With an oversized leather purse containing my weekend paraphernalia (I felt an overnight bag looked too presumptuous), I headed to the airport washroom. There I coifed my hair, touched up my make-up, and patted on dabs of Fleur de Rochaille perfume. Then I bought a lush magazine and leafed through it over coffee. By the time José landed, I was demure and romantic.

Seeing him for the second time was as engaging as our first encounter. As I watched him and the band coming through arrivals, Paulinho spotted me and turned and said something to José. José leaned over and asked Paulinho questions, probably "How does she look?" He probably asked in Spanish. José always liked a visual account. Soon enough our hands were locked, and we boarded the limo for the motel close to the CFTO-TV studios.

The usual spirited joy from the front desk staff awaited us as José began to kid around, tell jokes, and put everyone at ease. He always held my hand and never forgot to introduce me. He'd pull me forward and say, "This is Colleen."

If I left his side for a moment, perhaps to get a pop or an ashtray, I would see his hand reach back. He would start calling out for me. It was wonderful to be wanted and needed. When I said things he liked, he was quick to tell anyone around us, "Listen to her. She's got class and I've got crass. That's why we get along so well."

I liked his spark and his music. Mostly, I liked being with him at any hour, twenty-four hours a day.

At the studio, it was exciting to witness the taping of the show with the barrage of lights, cords, cameras, and crew. Watching the taping, I did miss the eye contact one usually has with another. I knew the impact that glances have to ignite and stir the flames of desire.

José wasn't able to see my expressions of joy, the excitement and passion I felt as I stood watching the taping. It was up to me

147

to verbalize what my eyes were saying. This was not so easy. In those shy, early days I stumbled through words precariously, careful not to get into adulation overload. He was so gifted, so talented, so connected to his art, and I was dating him. It was surreal.

Daydreaming on how to greet José when the taping was finished, I was stirred to reality when the wife of Kenny Rogers introduced herself.

"Hi, Mrs. Feliciano," she said with a welcoming outstretched hand. "I'm Marianne Rogers."

I smiled, shook her hand, and stated, "I'm not Mrs. Feliciano. My name is Colleen Riley." Her hand went limp, her smile disappeared, and so did she.

Bitch. How dare she. I was indignant. There I was, invisible again. I wouldn't have it. In that instant the crux of our relationship was seeded. As enchanting and compelling as José was and in the event that we fell in love, I swore I would never be Colleen Feliciano. I was on a quest for an identity of my own.

I had already been in weekly psychiatric sessions for two years, and I was uncovering the mental trash I let build up inside. I filled up with tears whenever I felt any kind of rejection. Smart as I was as a young business woman, my emotional self stood front and center in a catatonic pose if I was challenged. Through therapy I hoped to discover a way for people to like me because of who I was and not because I held an Executive Pass for Mosport, hung with the top

Canadian fashion designer, or dated a famous person. I wanted to be liked just for me.

That incident did nothing to disturb the magic hold José had on me. After the taping, just the touch of his hand pulled me out of my fear of rejection. We were soon off to Marilyn's for a spaghetti dinner with friends. I had prepared the sauce so Marilyn just had to cook the noodles. A great designer, she hadn't discovered the joy of cooking. The noodles were all lumped in the center of the frying pan.

"Frying pan! You cooked the noodles in a frying pan?" José sang out with laughter.

But after a few drinks and with José's fabulous music blaring in the background, the hungry guests chuckled their way through the lumpy dinner. José teased Marilyn for years.

While José was in Toronto, the last of the fall leaves were disappearing, and José and I took walks around the park on those late November days. He told me how much he liked horseback riding, and how he built his career in the coffee houses of New York. He talked about the long tours that consumed him about 270 days of the year. When he was off the road, he was busy recording. He was deeply committed to his music and continued to practice several hours a day, holding me mesmerized while the strings of "Malaguena" bounced through the air.

Sharing breakfasts and dinners in hotel restaurants with his manager and band members was like being with my old gang again.

Cutting up José's bacon strips or steak dinners, laughing at his jokes and one-liners, and listening to the road stories, it was easy to feel he was the missing part of me. As complicated as the relationship might be, I felt good when I was with him. It was better than I had ever felt in my life. I left morality out of the equation.

José quickly initiated me into the fun of being on the road by having me act as a telegraph operator one night. Around 10:00 p.m., José's bassist, Teddy Arnold, popped by our room to update us on his activities.

The girl from New York he wanted to see wasn't able to make it, so he had called another friend in Detroit. She would be arriving around 11:00 p.m. We agreed to meet with them for a drink, and Teddy left.

"Why don't you call Teddy's room and act as a telegraph operator?" José said. We schemed out the details and I called Teddy's room.

"Hello," I said. "This is CN Telegraph with a message for Mr. Teddy Arnold. Is this Mr. Arnold?"

"Yes," Teddy said. "This is Teddy Arnold."

"The telegram reads, 'Hi Teddy. Plans changed. Can meet you. Am flying up. Arriving 12:00 p.m. tonight. Love Sandra,'" or whatever her name was. Two minutes later Teddy knocked on our door.

"Come on in, Teddy," I said. "What's up?"

"Yeah. What's happening, man?" José asked.

"José," Teddy said. "I'm in big trouble. Sandra just sent a telegram saying she changed her plans, and she'll be here at midnight. What am I going to do?" Teddy was walking around our room frantically as he spoke.

José couldn't get out a sentence without laughing. Teddy looked at me. "You. You called in that telegram," he said. His tension disappeared, and we all laughed.

With Christmas coming, I hand stitched a white and black patterned Canadian maple leaf shirt for José and mailed it to Paulinho to get it to him. Ah, love. Marilyn and I were doing a Canadiana promotion for a retail store and came across a bargain buy of maple leaf fabric for only twenty-five cents a yard. The catch was that we had to buy all 2,000 yards of it. With tons of fabric left over, we made gifts for everyone that Christmas. A caftan, an apron, a Christmas stocking, and the shirt were all made from the maple leaf fabric.

Paulinho responded right away, telling me how much José liked his shirt and especially the perfume-drenched note that came with it.

The next time I saw José, he had two new pastel, tailored shirts copied from the style I sent him. That felt good.

Even when José wasn't in town, I always had exciting things to do. For this Christmas season, I was invited to an authentic Charles Dickens Christmas feast staged by Andre and Bill Coffman. I was costumed as "Nancy" from *Oliver Twist* and had my picture in a full page story about the event by the *Toronto Star* newspaper. My buddy, Walter Jamieson, escorted me and was handsomely turned out in Victorian garb. Walter was José's longtime friend, and we talked the night away about all the idiosyncrasies of the affair I was having. Walt, like me, could take every little detail and discuss it for hours. He was my Canadian counterpart to Paulinho and my steadfast anchor. He listened without judgment and always encouraged both my creativity and my heart to chart its own course.

In January 1972 José was touring but managed to call me a few times from Orange, California. He and Hilda had built a house just outside of Los Angeles. He was using one of their vacated investment properties as his sanctuary, and we spent long hours on the telephone. There was no promise in sight of when we would see each other and no talk of an impending divorce. It was just us on the phone for that moment in time. I wanted to seem him, but my dreams were fading fast. This was not like dating the boy next door. I didn't hear from him again until March 4, 1972 via a letter I received from Paulinho:

"We just came back from a long tour: Mexico City, London, Manchester, Brighton (England), Brussels, Copenhagen, Stockholm, Oslo, Berlin, Frankfurt, Dusseldorf, Stuttgart, Munich, and Hamburg. The tour was wonderful with all concerts SOLD OUT everywhere (two shows). José is very, very successful in Europe. In Scandinavia he is a Super Star with many albums (LP) on the charts (Hit Parade) and Che Sara (Shake a Hand), the San Remo song from last year is a big hit all over the place. It's #1 in some countries - #2 in others and so on. It's unbelievable to see people trying to get tickets outside and crushing windows and doors in a riot. I'm very happy and proud of José, he deserves the best. We talked about you on the tour. Heading out on another tour of Israel, South Africa, New Zealand, Japan, Philippines Island, Hawaii and back to LA for May 22nd. Sorry about my English, love, peace, Paulinho."

I was excited to receive the letter, but it was obvious that the heavy tour schedule precluded my being able to see José soon. Advice from friends poured in. Mostly I was told to be right there beside him as much as possible. Travel to his shows and be persistent.

My son was ten years old. I was running a small business. My place was in Toronto with my child and my business. It was up to me to make my life interesting, and up to José to call me if he wanted to see me. I was certain I wouldn't be chasing José around the world in the hopes that he would be glad to see me. What did I know about "cherche l'amour" anyway? What I was trying to do was be a good mom.

Penned Moments revisited

Vs.1

SUPERSTAR @1972 Colleen Riley CAPAC
I fell in love with a superstar

But he was always traveling far

And in my life he couldn't play a part

He'd see me when he came to town

And we as lovers would lie down

And when he left he always took my heart

CHORUS:

Oh, we had fun and we made plans

And the things he said I would really dig

But the only times that they came true

Were just when he was passing through

When some promoter booked him on a gig.

Vs.11

He'd call me on the telephone

When he was low and all alone

And tell me just how much he cared for me

And I would stammer back and say

I miss you every passing day

I want to see you soon, when will it be?

Repeat Chorus.

In Paulinho's
courtyard on my first
visit to Los Angeles,
1973.

We lived above the Unicorn
on quaint Cumberland Street
in the late 1960's. That's me
in front with a mini skirt.

Me at Citation Motors
about to step into a
2+2 Ferrari.

The manager of Peter
Stuyvesant Restaurant in
Boston hams it up while Paul
Theberge and I laugh about
their fish specialty, Scrod.

Kitty's Toronto wedding. Her sister Aileen on the right. I'm in the middle.

Me in Kitty's backyard hammin' it up.

Paulinho Magalhaes hamming it up with José. Dallas, Texas 1974.

José and I in Dallas, Texas, 1974

José reading brailled lyrics
to learn a new song. Dallas,
Texas 1974.

My charity bowling
team for Big Brothers
– from left to right, Me,
Joyce Barslow, Linda
Shapiro, Anne Berkeley
& Phyllis Marshall.

Spaghetti at my house.
Left to right, Efrem's son,
Efrem, Marilyn Brooks,
Paulinho Magalhaes, Denise
Francoeur, son Robert.

Me sitting beside Don
McGivern, President of
the Hudson's Bay Stores
in Rafael's Apartment.
1978

Getting José prettied up for his show in the Venetian Room, Dallas, Texas 1974.

José and I in Toronto, Canada 1975 (in my afro curls!)

José and I in Toronto.

This was the creative night we finished writing my hit song Keeping You On My Mind. ©

Me with record producer Bob Gallo.

Our billboard to promote our record.

Friend Joyce Barslow at my record launch party.

Uncle Palma, Robert and Me.

Actress Nicole Morin with Father Heffernan at our record launch.

Dusting off Jose Feliciano's Star on the Hollywood Walk of Fame.

Marilyn Brooks and I at the opening of a Toronto Hotel.

Aruba 1974, me on the right with Miss Canada, Terri Clark, in the middle.

CHAPTER TWELVE
BACK INTO MAINSTREAM

The tallest apartment building in Toronto, the 51-storey Manulife Centre, was nearing completion in the spring of 1972. Located at Bay and Bloor where stores like Tiffany, Chanel, and Gucci now preside, it boasted 781 apartments. The top floor was a restaurant and a tenants' deck. But most important, they accepted children. We were able to move into the building and back downtown near our old neighborhood haunts.

Midst the hammers, nails, and drywall of ongoing construction, we moved into a completed lower level unit in May 1972. We later moved to the 49th floor.

The Manulife complex was filled with stores and restaurants, and Sundays saw fabulous brunches at the spectacular Boulanger's restaurant. My other favorite haunt, the Courtyard Cafe, was just two blocks away. Between the two sites, I indulged my passion for white linen tablecloths. I enjoyed after-dinner coffee every night at the Courtyard while live, classical music filled the room. Most of my weekday luncheons were also at the Courtyard, many of them spent with the charming social columnist for *Toronto Life* magazine, Edie Frankel. Weekend get-togethers were usually at Boulanger's or another sign-of-the-times eatery, Crepes. At Cumberland and

Bay, Crepes boasted marble and wrought iron décor, slag floors, and an abundance of windows and greenery.

I love restaurants and went out for breakfast every morning once Robert was off to school. With a pen and notebook in hand, I would map out my day, sketch, and write poems.

My dining room was transformed into an office. Whirlwind promoter, Joyce Barslow was the next influential person in my life. She was the Public Relations Consultant for the Miss Canada and Miss Teen Canada Pageants, and she retained me as official biographer for pageant contestants. Once a year, for each pageant, the 29 or 30 regional winners from across Canada converged in Toronto for a week of pageant festivities. With great speed, I wrote not only a biography for each contestant, but also the press kit news releases, the schedule of activities, and the contents of the television special. It was like writing a pocketbook in a week. I had a small, portable, manual typewriter which I set up in the hotel suite designated for press and fashion activity. Marilyn Brooks was on one side of the room with her measuring tape and pins, wardrobing each contestant. Joyce took another corner and monopolized the telephone lines, and I sat cross-legged on the floor with my typewriter sitting on top of its own lid. We were all hysterical by the end of the week.

Performing around the world, José usually called when he was within a thousand-mile range of Toronto. Because his manager/wife paid all the bills, it was difficult to make calls that wouldn't show up on the hotel bill. Consequently, the infrequent calls were charged to someone else's telephone.

I needn't have worried about his calls that summer, however, because I was about to get crushed no matter how many times we talked. José had a gig at Ontario Place in late August. At Paulinho's request I rounded up Marilyn, Efrem, and Denise Francouer, a French-Canadian woman I had introduced to Paulinho. I was excited. Seeing José meant everything to me. I was like a mannequin until he stepped into my life. Then, I clicked on, and I was whole. For the first time in my life, I felt I was loved. Gone were all the fears of unworthiness. None of the ghosts mattered. Not when I was with him. So with great anticipation that this man - this drug for my soul - would soon be by my side, I was excited when I heard Paulinho's voice on the phone. They had just arrived in Toronto. After the usual greetings, his voice softened, and he said in his Spanish accent, "I'm sorry. José is not alone. He is with a friend he met in Buffalo."

The bubble burst. My eyes flooded.

"I'm so disappointed," I quivered while my interior involuntarily gulped in preparation for a massive tear attack.

"You and your friends must still come to the concert. You're part of the Feliciano family. I want to see you. Everybody wants to see you. I'll leave the passes. You just tell me how many you want."

There it was. José was with someone else. I knew he was still dating Susan. I sensed he probably dated other women, too. And

I knew he was having a difficult time at home. But we had our special relationship. How could he not want to see me? I let the tears flow. My son saw the hurt. What could I say to him? He was too young to understand. I just cried it out until it was time to go to the concert. My friends rallied round, and we took our seats to witness a terrific concert in the packed Forum at Ontario Place. It was a warm summer night with a cool breeze, and my heart pounded with every strum of José's guitar. With him or without him, I felt his magnetism. In his stage presentation, he talked about Toronto and how he was going to come back soon because there was someone he wanted to see. Please God, let it be me.

We went backstage when the concert was over and the wonderful, smiling, Paulinho dashed over to greet us. One by one, the band members came out of their dressing rooms. Their faces were filled with smiles as they saw me and hugs came flying.

Then Bob Drew, José's manager said, "Just wait a moment, and I'll get José."

He brought him over and said, "Colleen is here."

José hugged me. He put his lips to my ear and whispered.

"I'm so glad you're here."

I felt excited again.

Just then his dressing room door opened, and a young girl came rushing to José's side wearing a chintzy, long white satin cape trimmed with white marabou feathers. José let go of me and stood by the girl. It stung. It was time to get out of there.

Paulinho, Denise, Marilyn, Efrem, and I made our way to my place for dinner and drinks. Everyone told me to hang in there.

A couple of months later, José was back, and the summer night was forgotten. Together we had a late night dinner party with about twenty friends and industry sorts. We made up. José had a busy schedule ahead, and it was going to be a while before we would be seeing each other. We made every moment count. There was no news of his divorce. He was still seeing Susan. Time for me to get on with my own life.

CHAPTER THIRTEEN
THE EXCITING PUBLIC RELATIONS BUSINESS

In the early 1970's, Acapulco was the number one spot for vacationing, and Marilyn and I were on our way in February 1973 promoting the best of Canadian fashion. It was a joint project, with Marilyn as the leader and creative force and me as the behind the scenes administrator. We made a good team.

We created the "Canadian Fashion Caravan to the Sun," a showcase of Canadian fashions presented nightly for two weeks in a Mexican disco. The hot spot was Nepentha's, operated by Canadian entrepreneur Thomas Wayne, with his partners Patrick Young and Patrick's Mexican wife.

To kick it off in Canada, we offered champagne and strawberries around Marilyn's grand piano, inviting fashion designers to participate by buying into our promotion package. We wanted three designers to join the trip and were successful in getting Uncle John Burkeholder, Marion Cook and Pat McDonagh. The rest of the entourage included top models Lynda Hill, Kerry Jewitt and Cathy Reid, drummer-composer Efrem (Marilyn's beau) with his musicians, and Gillian Regher, Miss Canada 1973 with her chaperone. *Chatelaine*'s fashion editor Eveleen Dollery and her husband Doug Morrison joined us to shoot the summer issue, bringing art director

Evelyn Stoynoff and photographer Beverly Rockett. Last, but not least, the very talented "Scissors" as Marilyn called him - hair stylist Michael Kluthe. His sense of humor and sophistication added immeasurably to the trip. In total, seventeen of us headed off for the two week event. The Royal York Hotel hosted a farewell party in the newly opened Gazebo restaurant, treating us all to Margaritas to set the mood. The trip would culminate with a musical fashion happening in the hotel's concert hall as a benefit for the Women's Auxiliary of Big Brothers of Metropolitan Toronto, a community service organization for fatherless boys.

We left on a cold February morning, fortifying the flight with tequilas and margaritas and giggling our way into a sweltering hot and humid Acapulco airport. We anticipated trouble getting long-haired musicians into the country, but everyone sailed through easily. It was the new clothing we should have worried about as customs confiscated it all, including Miss Canada's personal wardrobe. Our spirited smiles faded as we conferred with our reception committee, Tom and Patrick, on what to do.

We presented all our documentation, including work permits for the models and newspaper ads. One ad showed that the wife of the Mayor of Acapulco was hosting the opening night festivities as a charitable fund raising event. Still, they refused to release the goods.

We offered cash. No deal. They were adamant. The goods were staying at the airport.

Worn down by our fruitless efforts, we left for our villa at the Club de Pesca luxury hotel at the far end of the Costera. We refreshed ourselves before being treated to a wonderful ocean-side dinner on the patio. Seventeen characters in Acapulco, a city that made everything fun. Clothes or not, I was glad I was there. So were the insects. By the next morning I was covered in small itchy welts.

There was no time to stress. It was my job to get the clothes released from customs. By 8:00 a.m. I was off to the government offices, stopping on the way to buy calamine lotion. Boldly striding past armed guards, I sported big pink dots of calamine over my chest and arms as I found my way to the Customs Office of Acapulco to see Inspector Camp.

The ceiling fans grudgingly circulated the dank smells of old floors that had been cleaned once too often. The hot, humid air pulled out the freshness of the perfume I put on an hour earlier.

Inspector Camp's secretary seated me in a row of empty chairs about ten feet from him. The offices were bleak with aged partitioning and dark oak desks. The inspector, a man in his forties of average height and build and wearing a dark khaki suit, fit right in with the decor. Defiantly ignoring me, shuffling papers, and making telephone calls, he kept busy while I sat waiting for his eyes to catch mine. This didn't happen until three hours had lapsed. Consultations with the secretary didn't help. The only person with the power to release the goods was sitting ten feet in front of me.

"Please have a seat. The Inspector will see you when he is ready," the secretary said again.

Finally, he requested I sit before him and sent his secretary to find an interpreter. Another twenty minute wait. He heard my story and said he would look into it. That was it. No action. No telephone calls. No nothing.

"Come back tomorrow," he said.

· The next day, I was confident we would have our clothes for the opening night show. It was being presented, after all, by the Mayor's wife.

A small two-door cab pulled up in front of the hotel at 7:30 a.m., and I sat in the front seat. Wearing a smart but provocative, low cut two-piece summer suit, I noticed the cabby's eyes fixed on my cleavage as I gave him the address. As we started to bounce along the boulder-sized cavities in the road, he turned and asked,

"Room number?"

I smiled inside. Of course he knew where my hotel was because he had just picked me up there. It was cute. I smiled and answered as if I understood him perfectly,

"Si. I am a tourist from Canada."

He looked over, his eyes compelled to take in the bouncing cleavage, embarrassing me, but it was something over which I had no control. He repeated with more drama,

"Room number?"

"Si!" I smiled. "Tourist going to Zucherro." The Zucherro is the market in front of the government offices.

In more emphatic tones, he tried once more before reaching my destination. "Roooom numbah," he desperately mouthed out.

"Si!" I said as I pointed out the market. "Zucherro. Gracious Senor." With that I paid the fare and gleefully made my way to the Inspector's office.

The glum tones of Inspector Camp, functioning this time without an interpreter, changed my mood. He told me about fashion promoters from Paris who brought new clothing into the country and sold it. This was against the law.

"We threw them out of the country," he said with great pride, "and told them they could never come back. Your clothes," he said with finality, "will not be released from customs."

Marilyn sprung into action when I informed her of the clothes. She elicited help from our team to dig through their wardrobes and surrender any and all new clothes so they could be used for the fashion show. Even designer Uncle John's new khaki suit was simply wrapped on the girl's side and belted for a sporty look.

Opening night was a huge success, largely due to Marilyn's great finesse in creative staging. Also a hit were the Canadian-styled bikinis worn with the hot new "bikini belt." The belts were designed by Rafael, who had recently moved to Canada from Yugoslavia, and was emerging as a new talented jewelry designer. Tom, Patrick, and the Mayor's wife sold out the show. The crowds loved Canada's beautiful models, the hot live music, the introduction of Miss Canada, and the three Canadian designers. The event had sizzle and color photos hit all the Acapulco newspapers, including a front page story in *Novedades de Acapulco*. There was still, however, the matter of the clothing our clients paid us to promote. We couldn't get our hands on it.

As part of the overall promotion, every evening we had a big dinner party in one of the best restaurants around, like Carlos and Charlie's or Blackbeard's. Gorgeous models attracted attention, and the seventeen of us fashion types made a splashy entrance, catching the eye of people like Johnny Carson. Our aim was to attract patrons to Nepentha's to catch the show. Acapulco was very much an impromptu place. The flow of its tourists relied heavily on what was "in" at that moment. All our dinner parties were pre-arranged. The restaurateurs could photograph Miss Canada and the entourage and use those photos for publicity. In exchange, we were treated to fabulous complimentary dinners for our group. On one occasion, we noticed an easel in front of a restaurant with a large photograph of Gillian Regehr and declaring "Miss Canada Dines Here."

Within days, the local newspapers carried restaurant ads promoting that Miss Canada had dined at their sites. It was very exciting. It was all win-win.

On the fourth evening, with Miss Canada still wearing her one white dress, Marilyn and I engaged in a tactical conversation. We were looking for a foolproof idea to get the clothes out of customs and on the runway. We would, after all, be compelled to return our clients' fees if we didn't promote their fashions.

Dreaming and scheming in an outdoor restaurant in the warm night air while sipping tequilas and munching on tortillas proved fruitful. We found a solution. We were there, we reasoned, with Miss Canada and her one white dress and it was getting dirty. Having worked with the Miss Canada pageant and trained in the Rafael Markowitz promotion camp, I saw the writing on the wall. Either the Mexican government release all of our clothing, or I would contact the press and put the "dirty dress" story on the wire services around the world. Now . . . how to effectively get the message across?

"Aha," said Marilyn. "We'll contact the Mexican Consul and let him do the work. It is, after all, a political matter."

"Great idea," I replied joyfully. "You call him."

"No, Colleen," Marilyn toyed back. "You call him."

"Let's have another tequila," I smiled back. "I need time to work out what to say."

I must admit there was one aspect of this whole episode that panicked me - the armed guards in the government offices. I had never been close to anyone with a gun openly slung over his shoulder. It gave cause for concern that we were going to employ political tactics to usurp the Inspector's authority. Of course, I didn't think we'd be shot for it, but I was uneasy.

The Canadian Consul was in Mexico City and was not expecting the emergency call I made to his home sometime after 9:00 p.m. I laid out the story for him.

"I'm not sure what I can do to help," he said.

"Well," I said in my efficient press tones. "Here's what's going to happen. If we do not have our goods released for tomorrow night's show, I am going to stage an international incident by organizing a press conference for the wire services. I will tell them that we have been in Acapulco for four days, and our new clothes are being held up by customs at the airport. Then I shall present Miss Canada in her one white dress, announcing, "This is Gillian Regher, Miss Canada 1973. She is stuck in Mexico with one white dress, and it's getting dirty."

"Yes. Yes. I see," his voice took on an official tone. Don't do anything. Don't call anybody. I'll be on this right away. Keep your appointment with the Inspector." He hung up.

The following morning I arrived at the Inspector's office to good news.

Inspector Camp informed me, "It seems there is a special law which I was unaware of until now that will permit you to get your goods into our country. Go to the airport after 2:00 p.m., and your clothes will be released."

I sensed this message was tough for Inspector Camp to deliver, but I was joyous. I shook his hand and thanked him before rushing back to the hotel with the news.

The clothes were picked up and readied for the evening's performance. To our surprise, Inspector Camp arrived and stayed for the evening to watch the show. Job well done, I thought, everyone on amicable terms. Wrong. The ball kept bouncing.

On the last Thursday of the show, Inspector Camp arrived again around midnight and seized the passports of the three Canadian designers. He refused to state why. There was a big commotion backstage. The designers were up in arms. The Inspector was cool while Marilyn and I aimed to keep everyone calm. Finally the Inspector told me to be in his office at 8:00 a.m. Friday morning. He left abruptly, taking the passports with him.

The armed guards still rattled me as I made my way to the Inspector's office. This time, he quickly ushered me in to sit with him and held up the three passports. His face contorted with disgust. He threw the passports down. He looked at me with anger.

"You Americans and you Canadians come to Mexico and contribute nothing. You drink and bounce all night on the disco floors. You care nothing for the Mexican people. You think you can do whatever you want in our country."

He picked up a different passport and flung it in front of me.

"Open it," he said.

Obeying, I saw a passport photo of Xavier Cugat inside.

"Yes," he said. "That's Xavier Cugat's passport. He thinks he's opening tonight at the Imperial. He's not."

I braced myself and tried to talk without a quiver in my voice. I needed to get those passports.

"We love your country, Inspector Camp. That's why we're here. We're showing our Canadian fashions and photographing the clothes in these beautiful surroundings. These pictures will appear in Canadian magazines and will promote your country."

His look was still harsh. I kept on smiling.

"But, you see. We're leaving early Monday morning, and we need those passports."

"Yes. You need them," he grimaced back. "But you can't have them until these papers are signed."

With that he shoved three legal forms in front of me, all written in Spanish.

"Your designers are here illegally," he said.

"How can that be?" I questioned.

"I saw the show," He speedily retorted. "They are stars from your country."

Stars? In Canada's barely known fashion industry?

"What is this about, Inspector Camp?" I pushed on. On this day, he was fast and efficient.

"At the end of your show, you ask the designers to stand up and take a bow, and the audience applauds. That is how I know they are stars who are attracting customers. Stars need a work permit."

"Well, what can I do to get the passports back?"

My heart was racing as fear swept through me. Marilyn and I were seriously out of cash. I continued to direct the conversation away from funding more work permits. Three of them would cost over $1,000.00. The Inspector made his final demand.

"Miss Riley," he stated. "I am on my way to Mexico City for a week. I leave at noon today. Your designers must each sign the forms in front of you stating that they are aware they have entered Mexico illegally. This may affect future visits. When you return the signed papers, I shall release the passports. If you're not here by noon, you will have to wait a week."

Bam! This was payback for the dirty dress story. The task was not simple. Acapulco is a city of nights. Our shows ended at 2:00 a.m. after which many headed out to the clubs or to party with friends. They didn't make it back to the hotel until lunchtime or later. I grabbed a cab and tore up and down the Costera swinging into all the beach sites and popular restaurants. Finally, I found each designer who, with great reluctance, signed the forms.

By 11:30 a.m. I was back in the Inspector's office. I was glad that this was over and glad that he was leaving town. He surrendered the passports and then gave me an apple. That was nice, a friendly gesture. I shook his hand and started off down the hall.

"Miss Riley," the Inspector called out. "Be careful. The apple is washed with Mexican water."

With not much time to ponder our fate, we were soon back in Toronto staging the return charity show for Big Brothers. It was a huge success. On the heels of all this activity, I went right into the press writings for the upcoming Miss Teen Canada pageant.

I was working at home, and the apartment was flooded with 8x10 glossies of teen contestants. My son Robert was quick to jump in at his level. He staged a hilarious, comedy pageant for his 29 classmates at Jesse Ketchum Public School. Eight boys and two girls were bannered with the names of each of Canada's ten provinces. With Robert as MC, the entourage was garbed in women's clothes with balloons and oranges bouncing around their bust lines. The event led to an invitation for the class to attend a pageant rehearsal. But the invitation led to an outcry from the burgeoning feminist movement for equal time in front of the students. Within days a student/parent forum was organized and a debate ensued in the classroom between the new Miss Teen Canada, the pageant promoter Joyce Barslow, and a feminist speaker. I loved all the activity around the pageants. I saw pageants as a path that pretty girls could choose to win fabulous prizes, attend great dinner parties, and travel. I considered choice important. Swimmers swim, runners run, and pretty girls pretty up.

With spring approaching, restaurateur Tony Amodeo contacted me. Tony was famous for opening a restaurant called Mister Tony's, an upscale establishment at the corner of Cumberland and Bellair in Yorkville. One of its most distinguishing features was a menu printed without prices. "If you need to know the price, you probably can't afford to eat here," was the attraction for Toronto's elite. It worked. After his success, Tony went into restaurant consulting. His newest contract was with the soon-to-open Macedonian Village on Danforth Avenue. Aimed at simulating an authentic Macedonian dining room, it boasted a huge room sufficient to serve 200 dinner guests. The interior was filled with pictures, treasures, and mementos from Macedonia, including a large painting of Goetzy Delce, a national hero who led an uprising in 1915. Rich wooden beams added a wholesome inn-like touch, and a large dance floor centered the room.

I worked with charismatic lawyer James Karfilis to secure the promotion contract. With James and Tony, we planned to stage a splashy opening night and pack the place with politicians, celebrities, and local personalities. Olga Sandolowich was to present the folklore dance group Selyani, and a four piece Macedonian band would keep the music going all night. Our popular mayor, David Crombie, was invited to cut the ribbon for the official opening. As guests entered, they received imported Macedonian soil spooned out of two large urns and wrapped in traditional hand-woven serviettes. There were suspicions, however, that the urns contained Toronto soil from Jimmy's backyard, but on with the event.

The day arrived, the restaurant looked fabulous, and the two hundred or so guests arrived on time for the dinner. Proudly at 7:00 p.m., the Mayor cut the ribbon. James and actress Nicole Morin scooped out the first spoonful of soil, carefully placed it into a serviette, tied it up tightly, and presented it to the Mayor. With earth in hand, for all, it was on with the dinner party. The night was complete with the help of a chef flying in from Macedonia that evening at six-thirty p.m. However, at seven p.m. the chef's plane had not yet landed. In the kitchen, the huge old countertop grills were filled with chopped meats, peppers and the like. Three assistant chefs stood waiting for the arrival of the head chef to prepare a feast for two hundred people. Seven-thirty came. No chef. Eight o'clock came. No chef.

Finally, at eight-thirty, the guest chef made his way into the room. Mister Tony announced,

"Ladies and gentlemen. I know you're hungry, and I'm pleased to announce that the chef has just arrived from Macedonia. His kitchen staff await him, and dinner will soon be served." The news brought great applause.

Back to the kitchen. Introductions made, the chef ordered the grills turned on, and all systems go. Within minutes the exhaust systems backfired. The vents had not been cleaned out. Years of dust and ashes dumped onto the grills and all the freshly chopped food. Everything had to be picked up and thrown away. Then a new meal had to be started. Dinner was going to take hours. Management told me to keep everyone happy. Tony told them to keep serving more wine. Between the two of us, we kept the party jumping.

In the restaurant, everything flowed beautifully. With the food catastrophe kept under wraps, we flowed through the room greeting each of the guests. We made sure their wine glasses were full and told them that dinner would be coming soon. By ten o'clock the noise level had doubled, but everyone was bright, smiling, had rosy cheeks, and was engaged in spirited chatter. By ten thirty, city official Karl Jaffary and his party became annoyed over the lack of food. Prudently, James reserved a table for four at a posh downtown restaurant he owned and sent them there by cab.

After Jaffary's departure, the crowd linked hands to dance the Oro with Mayor Crombie in the lead. Most guests were reluctant, but I charmed them onto the floor. Soon the entire place flowed with snake-like grace, winding around the floor and in and around the tables.

It was a compelling sight. All hands were joined and held high. All feet were moving in unique, individual versions of the Oro, and all aimed for the majesty of Zorba the Greek while tittering and sometimes stumbling over a chair. What a party.

Finally by 11:00 p.m. the food started flying out of the kitchen. The ravenous guests stripped the platters clean and quickly made their farewell exits. By midnight the place was nearly empty. Tony, James, and I sat back and laughed hysterically. We had done it. The next day, the *Toronto Star* ran a great picture of Mayor Crombie dancing the Oro. The event was the talk of Toronto. It was considered one of the best restaurant openings that year. I always wondered what everyone did with their earth pouch.

Great news came in a letter from Paulinho dated May 17, 1973. José and the band had just returned from a ten week European tour, and they just found out that they were booked for Toronto on the 26th and 27th.. In less than ten days, I would be at the airport waiting for Air Canada flight number 790 arriving at 4:00 p.m. where I would see *him* again. I liked meeting him at the airport because it gave us extra hours together. Paulinho was hoping I would gather a small group of friends for a dinner party, which he emphatically loved. In particular, he asked me to make sure Marilyn and Efrem reserved Saturday and Sunday for a get-together. Whee! Lumpy spaghetti or not, we were becoming a family of friends, and I loved staging dinner parties.

But not all the news was good. In the same letter, Paulinho wrote me that José and Susan were still in love though he was in LA and she was in Detroit.

I tried to get José to talk about it but, that led into philosophical conversations about life or José telling me wonderful stories of being on the road. We were involved in a strange set of circumstances. The root of our relationship was a passionate, though not desperate, need for each other. None of it was easily defined. I was too proud to be jealous.

Sometimes I thought I was stupid. But mostly I felt that what existed between a man and a woman could not be undone by another. Either the feelings were there or they weren't. Nor could our relationship change the way he felt about another woman. A wife could drag him away so that I might never see him again, but if he loved me, he would always love me. And since I wasn't interested in marriage, I knew I could lose him to his wife or a girlfriend. Those were the terms. Without him I still wouldn't be looking for a permanent relationship. With him, I experienced the greatest sense of well being I ever felt. So dating him at any level made sense. If he called, I knew it was because he wanted to see me, and I hoped it was also because deep down he loved me.

For now, for this weekend, I was happy. From the moment we were reunited at the airport, we just locked in. Still getting to know each other, still sometimes nervous, we were none the less magnetized to each other.

The jewelry designer Sarah Coventry had just created a silver maple leaf pin to be presented by Miss Canada to 50 contestants participating in the upcoming Miss World Peace Pageant in London, England. Joyce Barslow and I, still representing the pageants, arranged for a presentation by Miss Canada to José. We organized a small gathering, including my son Robert, in the foyer of the Royal York Hotel where José was staying. I proudly wrote the speech for Miss Canada.

"Music is an art that transcends all national boundaries. It is a form of communication that reaches people all over the world.

"Sarah Coventry has created a World Peace Pin for me to take to England in July when I shall be representing Canada in the World Peace Pageant.

"I am most proud to present José Feliciano with the first of these pins in recognition of the determined efforts he has made throughout the world for better understanding through music."

A photo of the event was featured in the annual *Miss Canada* magazine along with the photos of Trini Lopez, Ernest Borgnine, Kirk Douglas, and Liberace.

The summer skipped along with various press activities. I was helping Richard Flohil at the Mariposa Folk Festival that was now staged at Centre Island, just a boat ride away from downtown. I was also having fun at John Lombardi's CHIN Radio Picnic, also on Centre Island. My friend Joyce from the pageants was also the promoter for the annual picnic, catering to Toronto's sizeable ethnic community. Joyce staged the Miss Bikini Pageant which drew huge crowds and hoards of press photographers from all over the world. A huge press tent was set up with a sumptuous presentation of ethnic foods, cold beer, and chilled wine. On the massive parkland at Centre Island, areas were designated for eating contests and spaghetti fests. Singers and dancers from Italy and many other countries performed, and outdoor beer gardens were popular where juicy German sausages were abundant. Oomph Pah Pah bands welcomed Prime Ministers and special guests. This exciting annual event went on for three days, and I helped out in the press tent and trailer. One year I was a judge for the dance contest with the likes of Sam "The Record Man" Sniderman, owner of Canada's largest record store chain. Since most of the traditional dances featured male dancers doing fancy footwork while the women did a one-two step in behind them, I told Sam he had to deduct points for every group where women weren't given equal time.

"I can't do that," he chuckled.

"Sure you can," I said.

I didn't know then that I'd soon be in the music business and banging on Sam's door.

By fall I was part of the volunteer Action Committee formed by the United Way charities. Action Committee members worked as floaters on any project that was failing and needed help. I was put in charge of producing a concert at Convocation Hall on the University of Toronto campus. "Bandstand '73" presented music stars of tomorrow: Robert David, Mr. Downchild's Trio, the Good Brothers, La Troupe Grotesque, Dan Hill, Myles and Lenny, and poet Duke Redbird. It wasn't a big financial success, but through the event I met Dan Hill.

Dan was a young, obviously gifted singer/songwriter who had been jerked around by RCA. He was out, tape in hand, shopping his songs. Folk music was in its heyday, and we met when Dan played at the Riverboat club. That night he sang the infamous RCA scourge that he wrote - much to the chagrin of some of the RCA executives who were in the crowd. In any case, his sweet, unassuming way and his talent prompted me to help him.

"You Make Me Want To Be a Father," a song Dan just wrote was compelling, and my friend Walt and I thought it would be a strong song for José to record. I made submission arrangements, and Walt sent the tape off to Paulinho. Dan was terribly excited.

He sparked my enthusiasm. Knowing that José's upcoming visit to Toronto was in early October, I invited Dan to meet with all of us for dinner.

Well, it was a bit bigger than that. Paulinho's birthday was October 4th, and I was organizing a surprise party - a festive, colorful Mardi Gras. Walt's friend Carol insisted on having it in her home. This was great because it gave me more time with José.

José had arranged to spend two extra days. He was like a kid about the surprise party. It was to take place on their last night in Toronto. Every time we were with Paulinho, José would lean over and say in my ear,

"Don't we have to go the store now to get things for the," and here he would raise his voice and spell, "P A R T Y?"

I knew Paulinho could hear him. That's the way the three days went until the event: excitement, giggling, and lots of spilling the beans. However, it was a great surprise for Paulinho when he walked into a festive room where about thirty colorfully dressed friends all sang out "Happy Birthday." The décor, the exotic Brazilian buffet, and all the people he had met since his first visit to Toronto in 1971 brought him to tears. It was worth the planning.

And in this crowd of people, a young Dan Hill was anxiously waiting to meet the inimitable José Feliciano. Introductions made, we found a quiet corner for them to talk. Dan's eyes widened with

186

joy. José, as always, was earnest in giving Dan all the information and enthusiasm he could. He heard Dan's cassette. He didn't think the songs were right for him. But he did believe they were right for Dan.

CHAPTER FOURTEEN
HOLLYWOOD, MONROE &
THE ACADEMY AWARDS

The Miss Canada Pageant was on tap for November, and once again my home was transformed into a beauty gallery. I loved it. Hand in hand with the United Way, we staged a Halloween Ball at the Palais Royale Ballroom on Lakeshore Boulevard West. It had a "Glamour of the Glorious Forties" theme, and we incorporated the Ball into the pageant week activities. In the rush of things, I didn't have a costume until the night of the event, October 31st. I didn't know who Sylvia Sydney was, but my movie buff friend Joyce suggested I wear the new oriental dress Marilyn had just designed for me.

"Just blanket your face out with white powder, pull your hair off your face in a circular puff, don the gown, and there you are - Sylvia Sydney, the famed forties movie star," she instructed. "You can be ready in an hour." My neighbor Rosemary jumped in to help. There I was, totally unrecognizable. This was devastating.

I arrived late by cab and rushed inside. Nobody knew me in the packed ballroom. Hoards of people that I recognized, but not by name, walked past me. No one said hello. My tiny red lips forced a smile amidst the great white mass covering my face, but no one smiled back. Only the gracious sometimes gave a courteous bow.

Of course, I forced my friends into recognition, but no one knew the likes of Sylvia Sydney. They were in good company.

Time to move on. I wrote a profile on publisher Joey Cee, my newfound entrepreneurial buddy, for *Music Canada Quarterly*. I signed a three month promotional contract with jewelry designer Rafael, and I took on two writing assignments for *Cycle '74*. One was on daredevil Super Joe Einhorn who flew over cars on his motor bike. The other was on James the Mystery painter who kept his address secret because he painted motorcycles for bikers. With the income, I left for a two week vacation on November twentieth.

It was my first visit to Los Angeles. José was doing the *Midnight Special* with Wolfman Jack at NBC, and I was staying at Paulinho's home. A friend I introduced to Paulinho, Karen Zorn, joined me for a week. She had already arrived the day before I did.

Within kissing distance of LA, the sight of palm trees through the airplane window touched me deeply. I could almost feel the heat of the LA sun warming me. Like I had with the bricks at Toronto Union Station, this began for me, another love affair with a city. Maybe I was influenced by José's "California Dreamin'" song or because he told me so often how much he loved California. Whatever possessed me, arriving in Los Angeles felt like coming home.

Karen and Paulinho were smiling as I made my way through the arrival gates, overdressed in my long, black wool skirt and wool plaid jacket.

Paulinho lived in a modest apartment complex of several low-rise buildings surrounding a pool and a hot tub. The complex was surrounded by shrubs and flowers. Located in North Hollywood, his mid-sized home had two bedrooms and was comfortably furnished in dark colors. Paulinho's presence furnished the light and the sparks. He was always active and always moving into the next moment with a story, a luncheon, a spaghetti dinner for the "Toronto Guest", a drive uptown or downtown, or a late night dip in the hot tub outside. He was like a brother to me, and we talked for hours together.

José was distant. My dreams of secret phone calls, clandestine meetings and passionate encounters faded daily. Backstage on the night of the *Midnight Special* taping, José and his wife Hilda (who had now changed her name to Janna) marched down the hall not even stopping to say hello to Paulinho. Of course, José couldn't see us standing around the dressing room, and Paulinho restrained me from announcing myself. I watched the taping with mixed emotions. I was, after all, still going to be in town for more than a week. But José never called. He was, you see, a married man. Instead, he wrote me from Johannesburg.

On the same day I heard from José, Noble "Kid" Chissell sent me a copy of his show biz column in the *Hollywood Independent*. There was my name in print. My name was in a Hollywood newspaper. "Colleen (Riley) was visiting from Toronto with a message from Joyce Barslow." That was it. There it was. Kid and I had only met on the phone but would get together on my next visit to talk about some business projects. I knew for sure that I wanted to connect in LA.

As soon as I returned to Toronto, I was hunting for clients who needed my services in LA. Ah yes, my new client Rafael. By January twentieth, when ice cold temperatures and snow-covered streets hit Toronto, I was back to the warmth of LA to do a trade show for Rafael jewelry.

"Please, please, please." I begged Rafael. "Let's do the LA Gift Show."

On arrival (two hours late due to problems connecting at O'Hare Airport in Chicago), I met with Marilyn's ex-boyfriend Efrem, and off we went to the famous Nicky Blair's restaurant on Sunset Boulevard. It was a known hangout for celebrities. Before I left Toronto, Robert asked me to get Sonny and Cher's autographs if I ran into them. Their show was his favorite. He told me that if I wasn't his mom, he would choose Cher for the role.

Sitting there at the bar, I saw Sonny with a group of friends. I wrote a note, pulled out my wallet size picture of Robert, and asked friendly Joe the bartender to take it to Sonny. Within minutes Robert's picture was returned with an autograph on the back. It was part of the mystique of LA.

With a few days on my own, I cruised the area around Pershing Square. There I saw the beginning of the crusade of the Reverend Sun Young Moon. A group of about fifty people had gathered to listen, and press people were lurking about. I sauntered over to the media and exchanged cards with a couple of the guys. Later I met with trade commissioners from Canada's federal and provincial governments whose offices were close. Ed Wehan at the provincial office was kind enough to give me access to a desk, phone, and secretarial services for any of my visits.

Rafael arrived on the third day with his U.S. sales representative Dick Salay and his friend Szabo who was sharing the booth at the show. Szabo had invented the "Think Tank," for which the eminent Dr. Edward du Bono wrote the introduction booklet. It was a creative tool for lateral thinking.

So we were in the LA gift show where the men are separated from the boys. The enormity of the convention center was overwhelming for us. We were used to Canada's trade shows which were about 20% of the size. We were ignored by thousands of buyers who cruised through the aisles. The only perks came when nerds from various universities came to inspect the Think Tanks.

Well, nix that. Rafael wouldn't be sending me to LA anymore. Nice try. Back in Toronto, we met with government trade official, Peter MacDonald, to organize foreign trade missions to the not so glamorous cities of Boston and Cleveland. We scheduled them for May and June.

Then the phone rang. It was Joyce.

"Would you like to take Blair Lancaster, Miss Canada 1974, to LA in March?"

"You bet I would."

Air Canada wanted Miss Canada for a promotional dinner in LA, and pageant officials extended the trip to me in the hopes that I could create publicity for the pageant. Although the Academy Awards were happening that week, pageant officials informed me they couldn't get tickets. I was determined I'd find a way when we got there. Blair Lancaster was petite, about 5'2", and was bursting with personality. She aimed to open a grooming school after her year as Miss Canada. She used every opportunity to increase her knowledge and promote the school. Her chaperone, Trish, was blonde, pretty, and had fine British manners. This was going to be a great trip.

We shared the flight with members of Insight Productions who were up for an Academy Award (but couldn't get us in) for a short film *Life Times Nine,* and our suites were at the elegant Century Plaza Hotel. I had organized a combined press conference and welcoming reception for late Monday afternoon and hit the phones early Monday morning. Saying I was calling about Miss Canada was like announcing a new mayor had been elected in Kalamazoo. Reactions might have been different if I'd spread Canada's name around the world with the notorious dirty dress in Mexico. Most people I met in LA didn't know where Canada was except north.

"Canada?" The editors said. "No. We won't be there."

Fortunately I had invited a host of other guests who were coming, so I started making calls to get tickets for the awards.

Everyone said it was impossible. Wolfman Jack's manager Don told me even that he couldn't get tickets and the Wolfman was up for an award. Rafael Markowitz gave me a similar story. I was hoping someone from the forty five or so who attended the reception would come through, but all doors were closed. However, the reception did produce a couple of television and radio interviews. I also got an invitation to the premiere of Canadian David Acomba's film *Slipstream* from singer Ken Tobias ("I Just Want to Make Music All Night Long") and his brother/manager Tony. Eli Wallach also invited us to see him and his wife, Anne Jackson, perform in live theater production. The week was filling up.

On the morning of day two, my suite now morphing into an office, I was determined to get tickets for that night's Academy Awards show. I wasn't sure what excited me most: going to the awards or calling Toronto to boast, "We have the tickets. We're going to the Academy Awards!" Looking out the window with the sun streaming on to the swaying palm trees, I felt like a big shot. At 33 years old, I had a fabulous son, was dating a rock star, was nicely dressed, was in charge of a week of promotions in LA, and was working from a luxury hotel. I leaned back, put my feet up on the marble table, and called Gregory Peck, the President of the Academy of Motion Picture Arts and Sciences.

I reached his secretary.

"You're who?" she questioned. "And you want three tickets for tonight's Academy Awards show, and you want to talk to Mr. Peck about it on the day of the awards?"

One hour later Blair, Trish, and I were in the awards office picking up our tickets. These were not great tickets, in fact they were at the back of the farthest balcony. But we didn't care. We were going.

Trish and I had beautiful gowns but Miss Canada's sponsored wardrobe consisted of plain polyester ensembles. I called the pageant who gave me permission to spend $200.00.

$200.00? Didn't they understand? We were in LA. We were on our way to the Academy Awards with the likes of Elizabeth Taylor and Paul McCartney. We rushed to Saks Fifth Avenue, picked out a size three gown for Blair, had it taken in, and picked it up three hours later. It was $600.00. I had the pageant's credit card.

That year, energy conservation was big in LA. Stores reduced light bulb wattages, and hotels stored their limousines. The hotel concierge advised that it was impossible to find an available limousine, but the hotel manager came to our rescue driving us there in his own car. Off we went with dreams of arriving to cameras on us everywhere. Accustomed to televised images of a limousine arriving and a star stepping out, we were surprised to see so many vehicles lined up. It was like a five star traffic jam. Stuck between all the limos (most celebrities ignored the energy conservation guidelines even if they realized it applied to them), we were all tittering. Eventually we moved up to the main entrance in groups of three across and about ten deep. The crowds, held back with wire fences, were bubbling with excitement and scanning every limo for the emergence of a star. About thirty personages stepped out of their limousines simultaneously, we among them, and we made our way to the wide walkway. The entrance was filled with hundreds of press photographers strategically positioned behind line barriers on either side of the walkway. As thousands of the movie industry's finest made their way in, decked out in the best fashions money can buy, I assumed my role as press agent. I left Blair and Trish to walk in slowly, as I rushed forward to the photographers announcing the arrival of Miss Canada. My message was barely audible due to the screaming crowds. If they stopped clicking for a moment to hear me, then within seconds their eyes rushed off me, many saying "move over." I kept smiling and moved along the line, but it was impossible to compete with the awesome parade of celebrities. No one took Miss Canada's picture. They didn't care that I put her in a $600.00 Saks Fifth Avenue dress.

Our grand entrance over, we entered the foyer party with our wide eyes casing the room. Catching our breath, we wove in amongst the thousands and found a niche where we could stand. This four feet of space landed us beside Paul Newman, Joanne Woodward, and their children. It was hard not to keep smiling. Broadly. Our eyebrows raised without comment. I headed to the male dominated bar to get drinks while feasting my eyes on Burt Reynolds (three feet to my left), Peter Falk (three feet further), and Paul Newman (to my right). Newman's wine order was being held up because of cork problems, and we started talking about wine. My eyes were trying to see in behind his irises. I wanted to confirm or deny whether or not he in fact wore blue contact lenses as was rumored.

"Those are not contacts in Paul Newman's eyes," I whispered to the girls on my return. "I studied them at the bar." We stood almost speechless saying "wow" a lot. A woman with upswept hair dressed in a full length, white, Victorian lace, high neck gown and matching parasol strolled in. She was striking. But not knowing who she was I asked someone.

"That's Linda Lovelace. She's the star of *Deep Throat*," he told us. We gasped. Everyone knew that *Deep Throat* was a pornographic film. The name Hollywood slid over us like a giant adjective. Minutes later, we took our robotic gaze to our seats to watch the show.

As far back as we were seated, we still witnessed the infamous streaker who ran across center stage just as David Niven was to introduce Elizabeth Taylor. Niven commented,

"Ladies and Gentlemen, that was bound to happen. Just think. The only laugh that man will ever get is for stripping and showing off his short comings." The audience buzzed with laughter.

The following day we met Noble "Kid" Chissel at the corner of Hollywood and Vine for lunch. Filled with great enthusiasm about everything, Kid talked about movies and stars and dance marathons.

After lunch, he introduced us to Robert F. Slatzer, the author of *The Life and Curious Death of Marilyn Monroe*. Still euphoric from the awards, we listened intently while Bob told us tales of Marilyn Monroe. He spoke of their relationship and how they first met in 1946 when she was a model named Norma Jean. He told of how he later married her, and Kid attested to the veracity of the story having been a witness at the wedding. Bob Slatzer, who was sitting right in front of us, was married to the Goddess of Sex. Hollywood seemed to be more than just a suburb of Los Angeles.

Our next stop was a few blocks over, Frederick's of Hollywood. Famous for provocative lingerie, their mail order ads for skimpy, lace underpinnings were known to anyone who read movie magazines. When turning to the back pages of the magazine, their ads left me with two questions.

"How do I tame the urge to send for a black lace push up brassiere with matching high cut panties? And "what would I say to my mother about a package from Frederick's if I dared place an order?"

The store in no way matched the fabulous fantasies of the ads. I expected fluffy, pastel-colored satin cushions everywhere and marabou stoles flung over every dressing room. Maybe there would be a few Clark Gable types standing around. Not so. It was just a functional store selling underwear, related lingerie, and sexy, but chintzy evening gowns. Still, I managed to find a black sequined jacket, a style then in its infancy, while fingering the lacy items. Lingerie had come a long way since I read Frederick's ads in my teens, but the lusty influences lingered. Their undies held the mystique that great passions would be unleashed when you were in the arms of a lover who would beg to surrender himself to you once he saw you in black lace from Frederick's.

"Yes, I'll take two bras and panty sets. In black please."

Blair, Trish, and I exited the store with our bags full of stuff, nervously laughing our way down the street.

I called Robert in Toronto every day apprising him of all the fun. By the end of the week, he was bursting with joyful news.

"Mum. Remember that old table with all the awful paint you were scraping off?"

"Sure, sweetheart, I'm listening."

"Well, now it looks beautiful because I painted it for you."

Pause.

"Where did you get the paint?"

"It was left over from painting my iron bed."

Pause. Adjust composure.

"Oh. So you mean my little antique table is now white and royal blue?"

"Yup."

"Thank you, sweetie. It's so nice of you to help Mom."

"Wait till you see it when you get home."

"I can't wait."

I flung myself on the bed and reached for my tight LA jeans. The only way I could get the jeans on was to lie flat, pull in, and zip up.

I threw on a top, put a pack of long, thin cigarillos into my purse, and went to meet the girls for a night out at the Whisky Howl.

CHAPTER FIFTEEN
KEEP ON MOVING

Between my psychiatrist and my personal physician, I was a mess. I had started taking Valium and Sinequan. The Valium was to calm me down, and the Sinequan was to alter my chemicals to help me stay that way. This may have been a mistake. It sounds like a mistake. My physician told me I should stop flying so much. Why? I told him to just prop me up and keep me going. That kind of talk from a woman on the move only caused him to shake his head. It was true that I sensed some health problems, but what did flying have to do with it. Personally I felt terrific. The launch into my own business was fruitful and everything I was doing was fun. I loved raising my son. But, hand in hand with all the joy, I was getting serious bouts of depression. Could it be that my imperfections lay in the single life? Why couldn't I be in a satisfactory relationship? Why was I dating a married man? I was guilty of breaking society's rules. I was guilty of breaking God's rules. This knowledge did nothing to change my behavior nor did the penance of silence. I knew I could never openly talk about my affair.

Sinequan was to clear the foggy window to my soul. It was to allow me a glimpse at the despicable person my grandmother contrived. It was to give me a clue to my behavior. Mostly I felt like a ball and chain had anchored itself onto my self-esteem. I was sick. I felt that I needed pills and doctors to survive. Best not to think about it.

Drugged or not, I was off on my first official foreign trade mission to Boston, Massachusetts in May 1974 to sell Rafael jewelry. The three day trip was designed for Canadian representatives to meet with potential buyers at appointments set up by the trade offices.

About fifteen other salespeople, all men, were on this mission. Federal Trade Commissioner Paul Theberge hosted a reception providing us with statistics on items like disposable income, average wages, number of homeowners, etc. He then spoke about the city of Boston and in particular advised us not to walk on the streets after 5:00 p.m. He told us to take a cab. The indoctrination over, he opened the bar. At this point I made my exit. I opted for a slew of magazines and room service over drunk salesmen. I settled in after I insisted that the two star (if any stars) hotel change my room for something bigger than eight feet wide and not overlooking a roof with steam rising from it. This was not LA.

Early on Monday morning, I was in the dining room and picking out a table to reserve for the next three days. A creature of comfort and sensitive to the sounds of banging dishes, I liked sitting in a cozy corner. I slipped the maitre d' a twenty, reserved a table for the next two breakfasts, and asked to be seated at that table if and when I called for lunch or dinner.

The buyers in Boston were not ready for Rafael jewelry. It was like presenting a four-year-old with a plate full of carrots and peas.

The meetings were all morning appointments, and they were short and terminal. They weren't buying then, and they wouldn't want to review the line in the fall.

I took the samples back to the hotel and set out to inspect the downtown core, hoping to find a suitable store to sell the line. Instead I found Filene's Basement.

Located two stories under their main department store building, the world famous Filene's was known for incredibly low prices for high-end merchandise and designer labels. The view looking down from the staircase entrance was awesome. The aisles were strewn with shoppers in various stages of trying on dresses and suits, and hundreds of people sorting through sales bins for buried treasures. I couldn't wait to dig in. Several hours later, I left with a few Christian Dior wallets, gifts for my son, and an assortment of handbags, shoes and clothes.

As I was fighting my way into my room with all the bags, the phone began to ring. Paul Theberge was calling and invited me to join him and a few others from the embassy for dinner.

"Yes, Paul. That would be lovely. I'll see you at seven."

It was a delightful night. We went to Peter Stuyvesant's boat restaurant at Anthony's Pier 4 (the Stuyvesant sank in the blizzard of 1978). I tried the scrod, a fish famous for its anonymous provenance, causing endless discussions about its origin. Was it shrimp crossed with cod? Everyone had an opinion, which made dinner fun. Of course, no one would debate it if it wasn't so delicious. Boston wasn't so bad after all.

The trip to Cleveland was coming up. This time I sent out advance press releases hoping to stir up some excitement in the media. It worked. Writer Dusty Pilot of the *Cleveland Press* committed to doing a story if I sold the line. Armed with this good press news, the fashionable Higbee's department store placed an order. But the people of Cleveland just didn't get the idea of Rafael jewelry, even with the incredible double page spread Dusty wrote. That ended trade missions for that year. Oh well, back to Toronto to break my foot.

It was on the eve of the day that Prime Minister Pierre Trudeau called the elections in June 1974 that my friends and I went for dinner at Rugantino's. It was there that I fell off my two inch thick cork-soled sandals and fractured a few foot bones. In the movies, I witnessed actors taking belts of alcohol to take away pain. Believing I had a sprain, I ordered a couple of double scotches. An hour later, I was sitting in a wheelchair in a hospital emergency room drunk. I was embarrassed as I sat there trying to make a coherent sentence.

"You sssee. In the movies alcohol takes away the pain. I jisst thought I'd try it, but idd didn't work."

Nobody was impressed, and I was sent home with crutches and a big cast. I was told it would take at least four weeks to mend. This was not good news nor, indeed, was the hangover I had the next morning.

Advertising giant McCann Erikson, located in fabulous offices on Bloor Street West, had just made me a deal I couldn't refuse. In exchange for my services four hours a week, non-cumulative, they gave me a furnished office, the use of all their equipment, and secretarial services.   My job was to sit in on client meetings and come up with ideas for publicity and promotion.   It was great.   I always had ideas.   They also sent work my way.   I had just settled and had all kinds of business commitments, and now I could barely walk.   The timing was bad, and I was forced to return to my dining room office in order to keep up the pace.

One of my assignments was doing press work with Joyce Barslow along with Barbara Grant for the opening of the Prince Hotel. It was a huge event for Toronto.   Two nights of openings were planned. The first was a sit down dinner for Toronto's social elite. The second was a cocktail party for about 1,500 people.   Hosted by Japanese investors, the planning required meticulous scrutiny while meshing two protocols: Canadian and Japanese.   In a dynamic promotional move, Joyce decided on a coronation.

"If we have a prince for a client, then let's crown him!" she chuckled.

A huge jeweled, fifteen-foot crown was made. With the use of a helicopter, the Prince Hotel was officially crowned just prior to the opening.

"You know what else we need?" she said. "We need a Japanese princess. Nobility will help with the prestige of the event." In a couple of weeks, a princess was found. She would be happy to be a guest of honor for the grand opening. And so began a funny press story.

The princess, as it turned out, was a princess-fifth-removed. To call her otherwise, would not serve Japanese protocol. As press agents, we learned to say her title placing the emphasis on "princess" while rushing through "fifth-removed," all the while sandwiching it in jargon about the opening of the hotel. Sometimes you just go with what you've got. But her title wasn't the only problem.

The reality of the princess-fifth-removed was that, while indeed from royal blood, she was married to a plumber and living in Philadelphia. The question was how to take advantage of the celebrity without the press actually interviewing her. The solution came in photographs of her arriving at the airport. She was royalty after all. The orchestration began.

To lend credibility to the arrival of this Japanese princess, Joyce had her flown from Philadelphia to Vancouver. There she boarded a connecting flight to Toronto along with the passengers who had just flown in from Japan. One could hardly ask the press out to meet a plane from Philadelphia. The next step was to entice the press to go to the airport. Barbara Grant, an immigrant from Great Britain, was put in charge of the pomp and circumstance.

Barbara started the press calls but was getting negative results. No one was interested in going all the way out to the airport because a princess was arriving at 4:00 p.m. that day. A new tactic was needed.

After years of growing up with the British monarchy who commanded attention every time they appeared in public, Barbara had a sense of royal protocol. She came up with the idea to tell the press that the princess-fifth-removed had given them permission stand on the tarp at the airport. Adopting her finest accent, and enhancing it with an authoritative slur, she began the press calls again.

"Yes, hello. Yes, this is Barbara Grant calling. Yes, I'm calling about the opening of the Prince Hotel. I'm calling to inform you that we have just received confirmation from the princess-*fifth-removed* who is arriving this afternoon at 4:00 p.m. at Toronto International Airport. I'm calling to say that she has, yes, the princess-*fifth-removed* has given permission for the press to stand on the tarp for her arrival."

The press tuned in. "Give me that time again." Or "We'll be there. Just give me the flight number." Barbara kept up the accent and style for the next hour. The princess-fifth-removed arrived with flashlights popping and the Toronto press standing on the tarp waiting.

Several days later on the second opening night, I arrived on crutches for the extravagant cocktail party filled with the social elite of Toronto. Most of them didn't know about the posh dinner party the night before. Many would have been devastated that they hadn't been invited. However, standing around in my long black dress and Frederick's of Hollywood sequined jacket, I maintained my own protocol and told everyone how wonderful it was to see them, adding,

"Of course, I knew you'd be invited. Your name was on top of the hotel's invitation list."

That summer, Robert and I moved into our new apartment on the 49th floor of the Manulife Building. I had to hobble around until late July when the cast was finally removed. Uncle Palma generously donated his time to lay the white wall-to-wall carpeting throughout except for Robert's room where Robert wanted an area carpet to match his antique furnishings.

The new home was perfectly laid out for us. On either side of the living room, we had bedrooms with our own en suite bathrooms. Robert already had antique furniture including a big old iron bed. I lucked out buying a fabulous brass bed with a lyre in the headboard from a bank selling off bankruptcy assets. The lyre was José's logo. The kitchen had space for a bar unit, a necessity for all the entertaining I did. One wall full of windows made it wonderfully bright, and the spacious living room welcomed a dining set as well once I converted the dining room into my office. With all the white carpet on the 49th floor, I called the apartment my ivory tower. Marilyn made sure I always had beautiful clothes, and I glided around my parties feeling like a princess (not-removed!).

José arrived back in Toronto for a show at Ontario Place on July 31st having just spent four days in Monte Carlo and then two days in Chicago. He loved the new place. He especially liked what happened on Friday night. A local television station, CITY-TV, started to run soft-core pornography, calling it Friday Night Baby Blue Movies. The whole city was agape, but most tuned in to witness what all the commotion was about.

The renowned Swedish Art Film *I Am Curious Yellow* launched the new programming, followed by films like *Pas de Deux,* obtained from the New York Erotic Film Festival.

"Come on Colleena, Colleena tell me what she's doing to him," José asked as we watched one of the movies.

My face flushed. "Well, she's . . . ," and I burst out laughing.

"Wait, wait. Let's listen," he went on. "Okay, okay, tell me what they're doing now."

"Well, they're . . . ," and I laughed again.

Then José laughed, and we couldn't hear the story line. Ultimately, José never knew what was shown on the screen. And, I wasn't going to tell him. He did, however, have a good imagination.

The next night after the show at Ontario Place, José and I were backstage when Miguel Maropakis arrived. This disco and restaurant owner had been my buddy for years. We had become instant friends on a Friday night when he dropped by Marilyn's place to attend a wine party.

"Hello, Colleen," he had said as we were introduced. That's all it took. Nobody says hello like Miguel. His eyes sparkle and a smile breaks through his prominent mustache settled nicely on his Mediterranean face. The words flow in hypnotic tones and dance around you with his lush Greek accent. Within minutes of Miguel's arrival, Marilyn slipped on her Zorba the Greek record.

"After a sip of wine," Miguel said, "We are going to dance the Oro."

"But I don't know how," I laughed. "Will you teach me?"

Soon a group of us were dancing on Marilyn's antique carpet. I loved the dance. We kept sipping wine, and we kept dancing for at least three hours. The beat was so drummed into me that for days after I walked with my feet crossing over in a slow, repetitive motion. That night, Miguel and I began a long friendship.

What surprised all of us at Ontario Place that night, was that Miguel was also a friend of José. When José heard his voice, he yelled out,

"Miguel!"

From that time on, now that Miguel knew my secret, we hung out at Miguel's restaurant whenever José came to Toronto.

A few days later, I was flying to Dallas, Texas to spend a week with José at the Fairmont Hotel. José had a ten day gig to accommodate the huge number of fans he had in the city.

Philip Wuntch with the *Dallas Morning News* wrote in part,

"José Feliciano, the singer-guitarist of rare musicianship, opened a ten day engagement and mesmerized the large audience into one of the mightiest of ovations." He closed with, "The show is a sure triumph. José was a record-setter in Venetian Room attendance during his 1972 visit. And from the way reservations have been pouring in at the Fairmont, he looks to repeat that success again. If anything, he deserves it even more so."

Paulinho met me in the hotel lobby and took me to José's suite where I changed into a swimsuit and went to find José. He was lying around the pool and stretched out on a chaise. I gazed at him for a few moments. He looked so seductive. The day was hot, the wind was calm, and water from the still pool vaporized in the air. It was a commanding moment. It was the first time we were away from the hustle and bustle of rushing from cars to hotels, to concerts, to interviews, to parties, to luncheons. This could turn out to be a remarkable week, I thought. I quietly sauntered over, bent down, and kissed his lips.

José was playing two shows a night. After the first show, we strolled down the hall toward the restaurant. José was barraged with beautiful, blonde, stylishly dressed young women from Texas. We knew about southern charm. We knew Texas boasted about their beautiful women, but we were surprised at their unabashed pursuit to get José into the sack.

A young woman approached José.

"Hi, José. I'm Sarah. I loved your show," she said with a lush southern drawl.

"Well, thank you. And thank you for coming," José held out his hand for a salutary greeting.

Sarah wrapped her arms around him, pressing her bosoms into his chest. "Listen, if you're not busy. I'd love for you all to come over to my house."

José reached for my hand, "Have you met Colleen?"

Sarah ignored the question and snuggled in closer, rotating her bosom as she moved. "Well, you all can get rid of her and come on over."

With that she slid a piece of paper in his pocket.

"My phone number and my address are on that paper. I hope I see you soon."

She wasn't the only one. Of course some just wanted to shake his hand and say hello. But many, every night after every show, approached him with a lot more in mind.

José garnered admiration and respect everywhere he went. On this occasion, a group of black women on the hotel staff started talking to José about food. From then on, all our meals were home cooked, and we ate in the staff cafeteria.

The ladies discussed the daily menus while we dined, and José would give his approval or recommend another dish. For that week, he was their baby, and they did all they could to spoil him.

On our first night we met three couples after the last show who invited us to a trendy spot for dinner. As they were upbeat, fashionably dressed and in our age range, we joined them, getting around to all the great restaurants in Dallas.

We were having a great time. I was able to see José perform two shows a night, and we had all day every day to hang out. One afternoon at the pool, actor Richard Harris stopped by to chat. Everyone was friendly. Of course, a lot of it came from José. He always had a handshake and a smile for anyone who came up to him, even the nut cases. He treated everyone fairly and equally and never embarrassed a person if they made a mistake. I was proud to be by his side. It was astonishing to witness a man who attracted so much admiration and respect.

He also had a serene side. He loved lying around silently while listening to baseball games. He would become totally engrossed.

"If you want to go out and do some shopping it's okay. I just want to listen to the game," he'd call out, knowing it wasn't much fun for me.

On Thursday afternoon as we sat around listening to the radio the song, "Alone Again, Naturally" came on. José confessed.

"You know that song, "Alone Again, Naturally." That's what my life is like."

He went on. "I know most people think I have a great life traveling around the world, staying in the finest places, and meeting wonderful people. And that's true. But at the end of the day, my nights are spent alone in a hotel room listening to the radio."

He said he knew how important it was to be out performing. He knew he had to travel to promote his records. He also knew he had a gift, and he would always honor that gift. He knew his life would be empty if he couldn't share his music with an audience.

"Colleen. I'm on the road 275 days a year, and I spend most of my time alone in a hotel room. I love music and performing, but life on the road is lonely."

We talked about what it would be like if I managed his career and went on the road with him. It was our daydreams talking. I would never leave Robert, and he was a married man. But we played around with the thought. José, a genius musician, was pouring out his heart to me. I was uncomfortable. I don't know why. I turned away in tears.

In time I spoke,

"I'm with you now, sweetheart, and tonight you're going to have two great concerts. We're going to have a wonderful dinner with our friends, and you won't be alone. Not for one minute. I promise you that."

As the afternoon wore on, the feelings I had for José intensified. It was a blending of my fantasies with an ounce of reality. It was like an anchor that had been resting on an underwater ledge that had just slipped down another forty feet. I was falling in love with

José. My heart made its own decision oblivious to the course it must follow. This was not an ideal romance, but rather a quagmire.

We were getting ready for the first show when the phone rang. It was Janna, José's wife. It was a short conversation.

"Colleen," José said. "Janna is flying up for the weekend. You're going to have to leave." Plunk.

It took a few minutes for the message to register. I was in the middle of paradise and being thrown off the island. My mind had already coveted each minute of the next three days. What do you mean leave? It began to sink in. Janna was his wife. She could call the shots. I had no options. I had to get out. I was powerless. I felt awful.

"José," I cried. "I don't want to leave you."

"Honey, I'm sorry. I'm going to miss you too, but I can't tell her not to come."

Paulinho came to the door decked out in a satin shirt for the show, and I let in him and his girlfriend Chris.

My eyes were brimming with tears. Paulinho gave me a big hug and asked,

"What's wrong? José, what did you do to my Canadian friend?"

José piped in, "I didn't do anything. But Janna called and said she's flying up for the weekend."

"Paulinho," I said. "Will you help José get dressed for the show? I need to talk to Chris." With that we left for the coffee shop. Chris calmed me down as I babbled on with girl talk.

"Do you love him?" she said.

"I think I do," I answered. "Well, I know I love being with him. But he's on the road, and I have my son to raise in Toronto."

"Well, he wouldn't be with you if he didn't care for you," she comforted. "Sure, there are bumps on the road. But if it's meant to be, it will happen."

We went back to the room as the guys were leaving for the show. Paulinho gave me a big hug.

"Don't worry, little girl. These things happen. We'll be back in Toronto in three weeks. Everything will be all right."

They made their way to the stage, and Chris and I were seated.

The lights went down, the music started, and José said,

"This is for you, honey." And then he sang "You Are the Sunshine of My Life."

Tears surfaced as I shivered in joy. He loves me. He must love me, I dreamed inside. I'm special. I'm José's girl.

It was hot that night, so José and I decided to cool down with a beer. We sat with our friends in a quaint club. In fact we had a few beers, something we rarely did. We were having a good time when, without a break in the pace of the conversation, we heard our new friend Peter say,

"I caught a nigger walking along the beach."

"Well what did you do?" his girlfriend asked.

"I asked him, 'What right do you have walking on this beach'?"

"What did he say?" she asked.

"He didn't say anything. He just kept walking." He leaned his chair back in pompous indignation.

"And you let that nigger just walk on the beach," one of Peter's friends asked.

"Nah. I walked up to him and said 'look, you nigger bastard. You get yourself off of this beach before I call the police. And don't you ever come back,'" he replied.

"And did he go?" asked the friend.

"Yes. He went. Damn nerve." He replied.

"You have to watch those niggers. Some of them just think they can do anything they want," his friend said. "Why, just the other day . . . ," he went on.

José and I were numb. We liked these people. They were outgoing, friendly, witty, charming and the eight of us had shared the last three nights together. José and I needed to talk in private. We headed to the dance floor. This was the first time we had ever danced.

"Colleen," José started. "Don't you think those people are terrible? I want to go."

"José. It was disgusting to hear them talk." I agreed.

"Would you have ever thought they were like that?"

"No. I can't believe it. They're racists."

"I think we should head back to the hotel."

The deejay spun a new record, and the Shi-lites started singing, "Oh Girl. I'd be in trouble if I lose you now."

José took me in his arms, both of us stumbling a bit from all the beer, and we began dancing.

"Hmmmm. I love dancing with you," I murmured. José held me closer and whispered,

"We've got all night."

Toronto was always a good city to return to, especially now that I lived in an ivory tower. But I committed to giving up my luxuries for one night and visit my son and Uncle Palma at their campsite. Palma owned a motor boat, a tent, and a pair of water skis. Every year he took Robert camping. They went to Lake St. Peter in northern Ontario, staying in the same trailer park each year where they had built up many friendships.

"No. Don't get an extra cot ready, Uncle Palma," I pleaded. "Just find me a quaint motel, and I'll stay there."

Bugs terrify me - walking or flying. Animals of the night scare me. Flimsy walls of canvas in a tent scare me. No, a quaint motel would do just fine.

Arriving in the early afternoon, I found the clear country air refreshing. The guys gave me a tour of the site and Robert showed me his skills on water skis as Palma drove the motor boat. We thought it best I check into the motel before they pampered me with a campfire dinner.

The motel was older, probably built in the 1920s, and furnished in laid-back cottage kitsch. We brought in the bags, and I made my way to the washroom. There, in the bathtub, was a large, crawly bug about three inches long. I sat paralyzed and breathed silently. I was in terror. There was no way I could sleep there. The sealed tent began to look good.

Cautiously making my way back down the hall, I shamefully lied,

"You know, Uncle Palma, I've been thinking it over. I'd really like to see what it's like to sleep in a tent. Now that I've seen it, I think it would be fun. Would you mind staying in my room? It's just for one night."

CHAPTER SIXTEEN
THE LOU REED SPAGHETTI SANCTIONING

With José's birthday coming up on September 10th, I decided to make the usual spaghetti bash into a surprise birthday party and sent about twenty invitations to our friends. José had a free day on Friday, a perfect night for a party. This time it was Paulinho who had to keep José's party a secret. He was much better at it than José.

My spaghetti recipe was developing. Over a period of five days, the sauce simmered for over twenty hours with spices lovingly added as time went on. By Friday, voila! The chef had finished cooking her sauce. I loved to see José enjoy my home cooking.

The party preparations were organized on Thursday evening. With experience from cooking unique cakes for Robert, I baked a special birthday cake for José with music notes in the icing. The next morning, I was off to the airport to meet flight #373 arriving from Ottawa.

José was excited about the spaghetti dig in. He was looking forward to seeing Walt Jamieson, Marilyn Brooks, RCA record promoters John Murphy and Scott Richards, and RCA engineer George Semkew, among others. But I don't think he expected Lou Reed of New York's Velvet Underground. Nor did I.

Most of the guests had arrived by 10:00 p.m., and I was busy in the kitchen spooning out bowls of spaghetti while José and friends were buzzing with conversation in the living room. A knock came at the door.

I opened it to find George and his wife Sandra with a couple of friends. One of them was tall, thin, and fine-featured with orange hair. The other was nearly as tall with long light brown hair tied back. Both were in jeans.

"Well, come on in," I greeted them.

"Colleen," said George. "It's great to see you. I'd like you to meet Lou Reed (orange hair) and his friend Roxanne."

"How nice to meet you," I smiled, trying not to fix on the hair.

"I was just serving bowls of spaghetti," I told Lou. "May I get you some?"

Lou paused for a moment, slowly looked my face over, and replied,

"No. But do you mind if I shoot up?"

"Well, um," I stammered. "Why don't you go in and say hello to José?"

George looked over at me with his cute "what can I say?" smile and moved along with Lou into the living room. Sandra took me aside and told me George had been recording with Lou all day.

Roxanne moved close to my side.

"I'd like to help you in the kitchen," she said.

"Sure, that's fine," I cheered on. "You can serve the pasta, and I'll put on the sauce."

As I was stirring the pot I heard the sound of a man's voice at the kitchen's entrance.

"Excuse me."

I turned to see it was Lou.

"Hi," I said a bit nervously, afraid of what his next question might be.

"Like, I just tried the spaghetti. And, like, it was good. And, like, I'd like a bowlful."

Well, this chef's heart just fluttered.

"Roxanne," I ordered. "Get this man a plate of pasta."

The two of us put a hearty bowl of food together, and he was off. What a team. For the rest of the party Roxanne stuck by my side helping me clean the ashtrays, refresh the drinks, hasten away the dishes, and put the candles on the cake.

"Attention, everyone." I called out. "It's time for the birthday cake." Friends gathered around.

"José, I know it's not quite your birthday, but this is a special surprise just for you." With that I lit the candles and everyone sang "Happy Birthday."

José was surprised and moved that we cared to honor his upcoming 29th birthday. After he blew out the candles he was inundated with personal salutations and gifts. It was totally unexpected, and he was overcome with emotion.

José could perform to a crowd of ten thousand people and appreciate their applause, but he wasn't sure how to accept this kind of caring. He was thousands of miles away from home and family. Yet here in Toronto with his new family of friends, he was moved to tears by their outpouring of kindness. With his dark glasses on, no one could see the tears. I knew because he told me as I sat beside him helping to open the gifts and read the cards. He was embarrassed about the tears, but exalted. With Paulinho close by, the two conversed in Spanish. Paulinho always knew what to say to José. And this time he could identify with the element of surprise. José was soon back to his old self, taking center stage and rhyming out puns – a game we loved getting into.

The next day friends called to say thank you for the party. One of them asked,

"What did you think of Lou Reed's boyfriend?"

"Boyfriend?" I said. "What do you mean boyfriend? He was with Roxanne. She helped me with the party."

"Exactly," my friend went on. "And you didn't notice she was a guy?"

"No," I said.

"Didn't you see the stubble from his beard?" She bantered back.

"Well, no I didn't. But her name was Roxanne."

My friend was laughing.

"Yes. She was introduced as Roxanne which is a girl's name, but, she was, a guy."

I was blushing, "Oh my God. Roxanne was a guy. Did everyone else know she was a guy?"

"Of course they did."

"So Lou Reed must have known, too?" I asked.

"Well, of course he knew."

I paused waiting to register this information.

"Well, anyway, Lou really liked my spaghetti."

CHAPTER SEVENTEEN
OFF TO THE RACES

In the fall of 1974, I organized a fashion happening with Edie Ohayon for his store e.j.'s fashions. It sold Paris imports like Cardin, Mic Mac, Christian Aujard, and more. Choreographed by Lenny Gibson at the St. Lawrence Hall, the happening included a series of vignettes with a breathtaking Paris street dance, showcasing supermodel Lynda Hill. She stood on a dimly lit stage under a Paris street lamp wearing navy pants, a navy and white striped sweater, and a French beret on the side of her head. Dramatic music let us know her lover would soon arrive to throw her around in heated passion. The press loved the show and showered us with headlines like "Vive la difference in style" by Joyce Carter and "A fun show with French style" by Stasia Evasuk.

Edie and my jewelry client, Rafael, were part of a circle of hot entrepreneurs in the fashion scene, and the two also enjoyed gambling. If memory serves me right, it was Edie who came by one day to Rafael's office while we were in the middle of a meeting.

"Rafael. These are my friends Jerry and Sam, and they have a hot tip on a horse running this afternoon at Woodbine. We've come to pick you up. We're taking you to the track. You're going to make big money," Edie gushed out.

"Who gave you the tip?" Rafael queried, and they went back and forth until all the significant information was divulged. "Bet on horse number four in the fifth race. He's the winner," they told him.

Sam was jittery. "Come on, Raffy. The horses are going to run in half an hour. We can just make it. And then we'll bring you right back."

"Okay," Rafael said. He looked at me.

"You can come with us or meet me back here in an hour."

"I want to go to the track."

"How much are you putting down?" One of them asked as we drove to Woodbine Race Track.

"Three hundred each: Win, Place, and Show," was the reply.

"Yeah? How much do you think you'll win?" he continued.

The guy shrugged. "I dunno. Two, three thousand maybe."

"You're really going to bet nine hundred dollars?"

"Hey," he said with certainty. "This race is a sure thing."

I sat there considering my situation. I swore I would never gamble. I lost in the tin mine and later in a penny stock. Frivolous spending, my conscience cautioned, was like taking the food right out of Robert's mouth. What the heck. I'd live a little. I put two dollars on each. Okay guys, I'm in.

Bets placed, I stood with the four guys in the bright outdoors just minutes before our race was to start. Between them, they'd bet about two thousand dollars. I felt envious. They'd be going home with thousands, and I'd be lucky if I won twenty or thirty dollars.

"They're off," sounded over the speakers as the horses bolted out of the gates.

Horse number four was near the back.

"Don't worry," Edie shouted. "He has time to move forward."

We stood with our eyes fixed on that horse. Going into the turn, his flying feet did nothing to advance his position.

"Just watch him on the back stretch," Jerry said.

We were watching. He was running fast but not gaining on the other horses. Soon they were at the top of the turn.

"This is where he'll move into position. Watch him!" Sam cried out.

We had an inside tip. We knew he was a winner. We were confident he would pull out to the side, kick it into high gear, and cross the wire winning by a length.

Horse number four in the fifth came in second - second from the last. No win. No place. No show.

On the ride back, everyone was uncharacteristically silent except for an occasional "son-of-a-bitch" comment. I felt smug. Son Robert had nothing to worry about. Mom hadn't blown the grocery money.

Soon enough I would have other income from a new client, singer and stage actress Patricia Dahlquist. She approached me to act as her manager. I agreed to guide her career to where she saw herself going: Broadway.

Patricia was striking. Above average in height, she had long hair that was thick and auburn in tone. She had a wonderful smile and was a "little Mary sunshine," always extending a helping hand. From British Columbia, she had studied dance, voice, drama, violin, and theater arts. She moved to Toronto in 1971 and was lead vocalist with the legendary Haygood Hardy and the Montage. She also performed in numerous stage musicals and a season of the Tommy Hunter Show, a popular country and western variety program on CBC national television. Patricia had been hired as a background singer.

Patricia's heart, however, was live theater, and New York was her aim. It was my task to take her from a background singer to the stages of Broadway. She was convinced I could do it and so was I.

I had a philosophy about approaching closed doors. Make sure you're welcome. To do this meant there was a set-up, something that one did in advance so that when an approach was made the person would already know who you were and take the call. This did not provide a certainty that a deal could be struck, but at least you weren't caught in a flap trying to pitch something to someone who didn't care. (Ah, memories of the promoting excellence of Rafael Markowitz.)

For Patricia, who had a great voice, I planned to make her a big Canadian recording star first, and then push her records into the

United States. In every interview and every press release, we would state that her real ambition was to act on the stages of Broadway.

"Then," I told Patricia. "When we go knocking on Broadway's door, when you're famous and your Broadway message has been heard on interviews, they won't say, 'Patricia who?' They'll say, 'come on in Patricia Dahlquist. We heard you want to perform on a Broadway stage.'" Yes, I was a dreamer, and so was Patricia. Of course my morale was bolstered when I wheeled around super model Patti Hansen (later married to Keith Richards) and her manager. They were in Toronto for a day of promotions. Joyce Barslow had booked Patti on all major television and radio talk shows, newspapers, and magazines. The day would culminate with a photo shoot by Gerard Gentiil for the December cover of *Chatelaine* magazine. The interviews started at 6:00 a.m. With a full day's schedule ahead and the services of Eric, the white stretch limousine driver, we set out to make all the deadlines, maneuvering from one end of the city to the other. My early training with Nicole paved the way for our many entrances. I took command of security officers, secretaries and other personnel announcing in an authoritative tone the arrival of *Vogue* cover model Patti Hansen, here to do her interview with so and so. By the end of the day, with the last assignment finishing at 11:00 p.m., Patti's manager said,

"Colleen. I'm from New York and have met all kinds of professionals in show business, but I have never worked with anyone like you who could get through doorways so smoothly and with so much finesse. It has been a real pleasure to work with you."

With those wonderful words swirling around, my confidence was boosted. It would help to get Patricia's career off the ground in 1975.

While I was at my desk creating a career for Patricia, José called. Soon after, Paulinho called. José wrote. Paulinho wrote. All this contact, to make sure I had the dates and times to meet José for a weekend in Flint, Michigan on November 23rd. José actually dictated a letter to Bob Drew. It was a first. It was a last. He preferred the telephone.

As José and I sat around in his hotel room in Flint updating each other on our lives, Paulinho arrived with an announcement. Susan's mother and father from Detroit were coming to Flint to see the show and hoped to spend some time with José. Oh, God. José panicked. After a while he asked,

"Would you mind disappearing for an hour or so when they arrive so I can talk to them in private?"

Whoosh. All the accumulated feelings of excitement about this trip were wiped out. I got angry. How could he invite me here and then hide me so he wouldn't hurt Susan's family?

"No. I won't disappear. If I walk out that door I'll be heading to the airport," I stammered.

"You're right, honey," José said after a few minutes of thought. "It wasn't fair of me to ask. You're here and you're with me. And

I'm proud to be with you." Unfortunately, I wouldn't live up to the dignity of the endorsement.

The family arrived later than expected and telephoned José on their arrival.

"I'm glad you made it," he said. "I won't have time to meet you before the show. But hey, why don't you come backstage and see me after the show?"

José listened.

"Fine then. I'll see you after the show."

When the show finished, rather than meeting José sidestage as I always did, I went straight to José's dressing room and got drunk. I believe it was on Tia Maria.

Sometimes the wrong chord could quickly undermine my insecure personality. Choice was at the root. If a person who was riding on my emotional baggage train was executing a choice between me and someone else and I was not chosen, I was plunged into insecurity. Everytime. Tears always followed. The suffering usually lasted days while clouds of depression blocked any possibility of clear thinking.

Hence, the fragile moment when José chose Susan's parents over me, as fleeting as it was, knocked me out of balance. The damage to my self-esteem seemed irreversible.

I plunked myself into an overstuffed chair in the corner of the dressing room and refused to give it up. When José arrived, I didn't sit with him. Instead I said stupid things like,

"I'll just stay here so Susan's parents won't know I'm another one of your girlfriends."

José couldn't get any sense out of me. When the parents were introduced, I was uncharacteristically unfriendly and aloof. I slurred my words and looked like a groupie nobody knew what to do with. Perfect. I just wanted to go back to Toronto and forget everything. What was I doing with him anyway? I hated myself, and I suspected everyone else hated me, too.

José was not a happy camper. He had never seen me drunk. It was a rare occurrence, and he let me know how mad he was. I looked for salvation in the morning. God I felt awful.

I didn't want to concentrate on anything except how terrible the hangover was making me feel. The activities of the night replayed over and over filling me with guilt. Nothing in the memories gave me a clue on how to find redemption. It was his fault for initially asking me to leave. Where was my Sinequan? When was my flight home?

We maneuvered our way through the balance of the weekend, but we were distant. I don't function well without a fascinating dream bubbling around, and without his approval there was nothing to build a dream on. I knew José was hurt. He had witnessed a side of me that was not pretty. He had always introduced me with glowing pride. Now he didn't know what to make of me.

When we made our farewells at the airport I was certain he vocalized,

"Good-bye" and internalized "and good riddance." I was depressed. I would have to live depressed for the next few days. Crushed, I headed back to Toronto to bury myself in work. I cried on the plane, reacting to the usual parade of demeaning emotions as they marched through me: the pain of feeling overweight, the pain of not having control over my emotions, the pain of viewing my behavior and falling into indignity.

But I did know that joy was in front of me because of my exciting career. I knew I could bounce back when my desk was cluttered with creative assignments.

CHAPTER EIGHTEEN
PLANNING FOR SUCCESS

Not many people gave José's first wife Janna Merlyn Feliciano (formerly Hilda Feliciano nee Perez) credit for the role she played in José's career. But I did. I never met her, but the few people I talked to who that had meet her didn't like her.

"She's all business," they would say. "And she carries sausages in her purse which she munches on in front of you whenever she feels hungry."

They spoke of her as offensive. She was easy to blame. She was eccentric, and she was married to and managing one of the world's stars. Although regarded as self-possessed and arrogant, she, nonetheless, cleverly managed José's career in a male-dominated industry. Overnight success requires pre-planning. Getting even a genius to the top, requires hard work. Keeping him there is harder.

I didn't want to give her credit, but it was evident it was due to her.

In 1974 José diversified his talents. He shot an episode of *McMillan and Wife* as a Latin guitarist and an hour-long *Kung Fu* episode, taking on an acting role playing a blind Mexican drifter. He performed as the first non-black headliner for Don Cornelius on the weekly, nationally syndicated television show *Soul Train*, considered the Black America's premier music show. He played lead guitar for Joni Mitchell on her "Free Man in Paris" song. He also wrote and recorded "Chico and The Man," the theme song for the popular weekly television show of the same name.

He performed his music in twenty-four countries around the world, including three behind the iron curtain. He released a new album in mid November, *And the Feeling's Good* and it was hailed by *Cashbox* "with some of the most evocative vocals to date." *Billboard* said, "This is definitely the finest effort Feliciano has turned out in years." José kicked off 1975 with a world tour and was booked to perform at Carnegie Hall on April 20th. His career was impressive. I hoped my foray into management would bring my artist even a tenth of the success José enjoyed.

As 1974 was ending I had not heard from José since Detroit. I wasn't sure if he would ever call me again. What a lousy situation this affair put me in. Even if he was at home thinking about me, he couldn't pick up the phone and call. I couldn't call him. Anyway, what if I could call and he just didn't want to hear from me. Fortunately, I didn't like wallowing in self-pity. Well, not for more than two days anyway. With New Year's coming up, it was time to put aside my personal emotions and move forward with creative projects.

To a great extent I felt complete sharing my life and my love with my son. Love always flowed from his warm brown eyes. Just a few months back when he saw me light up another cigarette, he could hold his tongue no more.

"Go ahead and light up that cigarette," Robert said. "But I'm the one who'll suffer. Because you'll be dead ten years earlier than you should be, and I won't have a mother." In a few weeks, I would be away on a promotional assignment in Aruba, enjoying a steak dinner purported to cost $30,000.00. Robert's comments would prompt me to give up smoking. But I could already see myself eating instead of smoking, watching the weight pile on.

Oh, oh. Life was never straight forward. There were always curves ahead.

Penned moments revisited

You talk and yet it's distant

Not like the days you were insistent

On caring and sharing

All in life that was daring

Your soul seems to be self-resistant.

But I'm still here and I need you

And can't we find a way

To re-string the guitar

With a melody bar

With no sharps and no flats when we play.

The End of Part I

EPILOGUE

It is now fifteen years since the force of writing demanded I write my life story.

The following epilogue is to show the elaborate efforts I went through to avoid actually writing.

The Writing Years

"Robert!" I screamed to my son on the phone. "NIKE is interested in my footwear designs."

On that cold January day in 1994, I received a letter from Nike Inc. requesting me to register my footwear sketches in Washington, DC and resubmit them to their company.

Maybe this was going to be my year. Although my thoughts had now shifted to footwear, I never lost sight of the goal of writing my life story. I was eager to write, but I was broke. My energetic hours were spent chasing down enough money to live on. I needed a literary agent to find a publisher who could provide funding I could take time off to write. Phil Knight, CEO of NIKE, Inc., was acquainted with the agent I wanted, and I hoped that doing business with NIKE would get me an introduction to that agent - Michael Ovitz, the Czar of agents in Los Angeles. That introduction was now a possibility. Maybe this girl born into welfare in Ottawa, Canada in the forties, who had lived with her big dreams, was going to make a dream come true. It seemed so simple. I believed all I had to do was let an agent know my story, which included a lifetime affair with singer/guitarist José Feliciano. The agent would rush to sign me, find me a publisher, and an advance royalty check would follow. Yes, delivered right to me in downtown Toronto, Canada.

I considered writing the book for some time. But when I was ready, the recession in 1989 hit and bankruptcy soon claimed a house I had bought a few years earlier and everything else. I kept my mink coat, a small diamond pendant, and a bottle of perfume. I ensconced myself in a bachelor apartment in the Sutton Place Hotel/Residence. This nightmare of poverty morphed into depression. All the while, music stations across Canada were making my song "Keeping You On My Mind" into a hit.

Shipped in what seemed to be the hours before the recession hit, the record sprung to the charts. My son and I had recently formed an independent record label, GCR Records (for Gertrude Colleen Roberts) and pressed three singles with Robert on lead vocals. Our biggest moment was when the first release caught on with radio stations across the country. *RPM*, a Canadian music trade publication, wrote a front-page story referring to Robert as the "new Canadian kid on the block." Music directors from across the country sent notes hailing the single. We were dumbfounded by the on air success. We started an ad campaign with the slogan "Let's Make It Number One." Our small budget was quickly wiped out. We needed promotional dollars to take the song up the charts and force a distribution deal so we could sell more records. We couldn't do it. Real estate had de-valued by at least fifty percent. Everyone we knew was in a crunch. The song went bravely onward to number 15 on the *RPM* charts staying around that number for six months. It was the longest chart time of any single that year and the only charted song without album support. All we could do was watch.

The song happened concurrently with the death of my Uncle Palma and a slip on the ice that cracked the coxzis bone at the base of my spine. Deep in mourning, battling with severe pain and facing poverty, I found it difficult to cope. Those inner voices that know so well how to tear one apart, fed me horror stories of my failures. It was a message from Donald Trump in his book *The Art of the Deal* that showed me how to get out. The message I remember is that we all drive to work facing problems. It's how we solve them that makes the difference. Until then I believed everyone faced problems with relative ease except me. I empathized with Trump and the feelings he endured when his dreams fell apart. It soothed me to wonder what problems Trump was facing that day as I drove along facing my daily fears. Although waking in a depressed state, I began to yell "Hallelujah" before rising from bed each morning. This took the pressure off. It was hard not to start the day smiling after that burst of joy. By 1992, a creative drive became my reality once again, and I moved forward with the planning stages of the book. By 1993 I had written an outline, a list of ideas, and a few sample chapters.

At the bookstore, I perused the best selling autobiographies. I took the names of ten top New York publishers and sent them a note about my summary and my twenty year affair with José. Somehow we had a love affair that would never see us together and yet never see us part. I was driven to write my life story not because of José but rather because of my years of therapy. I was certain the news that I was ready to write it would be warmly received. The joy I felt as the mailbox closed, sending off my letters to publishers, was incredible. It was for me a *fait d'accompli*, a job accomplished. My fate was set. I fantasized a host of publishers banging on my door. My friends didn't call me "Miss Rose-Colored Glasses" for nothing. And when it involved my personal dreams - make those glasses a pair of doubles!

Only two publishers replied, indicating I needed an agent if I wanted to get my material read. One sent a list of 500 names from which I chose about 25 to whom I sent a flyer. A few responded that they simply do not read unsolicited material, and they weren't soliciting mine. I felt that there was no way in.

Pikers, I thought. I set out to find out who was the absolute best agent in Los Angeles.

It wasn't long before the Hollywood magazines led me to Michael Ovitz of Creative Artist's Agency. I called producer/friend Michael Steele.

"What is going on, Michael? I sent an inquiry to Michael Ovitz about being my agent, and it came back marked 'unsolicited and unread'."

"That's the way it is, kiddo." Michael stated. "In LA they are just swamped with mail from wannabes. Believe me, Colleen. I've been in their offices, and they literally have hallways filled with three-tiered carts packed with unsolicited queries, movie scripts, manuscripts, outlines, and brown envelopes stuffed with papers. You really need to be connected."

Humph! This was not an answer I liked. Leaving the rose-colored glasses on, I called Mike Ovitz in LA and reached his secretary. I did my patter about having an outline for my book and may I have permission to send it.

Her air was immediately haughty. "No, we do not accept unsolicited manuscripts."

"Well, when you do accept a manuscript by what method does it come through your door?"

"You will need an 'introduction' from an agent or a lawyer."

"So, if my lawyer sends you an introductory letter, I'll be able to get my manuscript to you?"

"No. It has to be from a lawyer we do business with."

"Good then. Please give me the name of your lawyers."

"I can't do that." She struck the final blow.

I've never been sure if it's the fire of the Irish in me or the tenacity of the French on my mother's side that sometimes takes me to my greatest heights of imagination. I do know that on that day I swore that if they wanted an introduction, by God I would create one.

Not long after, friend Kennedy Coles, who married Marilyn Brooks in 1982, called to tell me about a story in the August 1993 issue of *Vanity Fair*. The article indicated that Phil Knight and Michael Ovitz had met to discuss promotional ideas.

That's it, I hummed inside. I'll come up with promotional ideas for NIKE, and if they like them I'll insist that my payment include an introduction to Mike Ovitz. I dreamed of the setting. We would meet for lunch at Daisy's in Beverly Hills.

Phil Knight would say to Ovitz, "I want to introduce you to someone." Then I would say to Mr. Ovitz,

"I am negotiating a contract with NIKE for my designs and I want you to be my agent. Your secretary said I needed an introduction. Does this suit your criteria?" Then we would all laugh and have a great lunch.

Shine the glasses! It wasn't all pipe dreaming. Not from my creative side, in any case. I am an idea person, and I knew I could create something for NIKE.

A few days later, the promotion idea switched to product ideas when I read that NIKE sales were running second to IBM, and they were looking to expand their product line. Bingo. Within twenty-four hours, I designed the NIKE chair complete with laces running up the side of the cushions. The idea was to have the definitive computer chair, the one design that beat all, the chair to bring comfort to a five-foot tall secretary or a seven-foot tall basketball player. I even laid out the ad campaign. I drew a rough sketch of the proposed shoelace chair and added, "If your feet feel good, how's your back? Now your computer's running, and NIKE is still there to support you."

I sent the idea off with a letter to Phil Knight, with words like "already up there with IBM, you could take a seat alongside them," and "Maybe you would consider hiring me as a freelance consultant to come up with ideas. I'm quite good at it." The depression was definitely lifting with every new inspiration.

NIKE wrote back that they were only looking for footwear and athletic apparel designs, and I was welcome to submit ideas.

I'm not quite sure if I owned a pair of running shoes, but I did understand comfort. I hoped someone would create sneakers that didn't look like sneakers. Now, I faced the challenge. Within a few days I created "Magic Movers," lush-looking comfort shoes and boots created out of leather-trimmed ancient carpet designs with the message, "Can you believe there's a NIKE under there?" I gathered a collection of old auction catalogues, cut out miniature prints of wonderful carpets, and pasted them into my hand sketched footwear designs. Voila! The idea to take a "magic carpet" ride with NIKE footwear was born. Son Robert suggested carpeted insoles. Hand sketched and patch pasted on 11" x 17" paper, I sent off the designs.

In January, 1994 NIKE expressed an interest to review the designs but only after legal registration. Once registered and mailed, I waited with great anticipation for the next few months while my focus on people shifted from their eyes to their feet. I was back to focusing on my writing.

There was an aspect of the book that was going to be difficult - telling José about it. He was a married man and a private person. My friends warned me he would never see me again after I told him. I was so self-consumed that I believed he would be happy. I believed we were heading to a more permanent relationship. I believed the book would act as the catalyst for that big move on our journey to the last chapter - the one that reads "and they lived happily ever after." I had waited all my life to be a writer, putting the talent aside when I was twenty years old to raise a son on my own. Now I was ready. I never knew I'd be compelled to write non-fiction, let alone the story of my life. But that was my creative path, whether I liked it or not, writing it was my focus.

José was playing at an auditorium in Brantford, Ontario and called me to join him there. It was a cold November morning (so much happens to us in Novembers), and we were just waking. Soon he would be flying off, and I knew I had to tell him. "José," I started gently, "I'm going to write a book about the story of my life."

His body stiffened. "Am I in it?"

I giggled a bit. "Well of course you are. It's my life story."

"What am I doing in it?" he asked.

This was not going well. I wasn't hearing any encouragement. Nor did I understand his question.

"You're in it because you're the man I love," I said.

José turned away from me, climbing into a sullen world. The room was still. The fragile soul of the artist within me backed away in remorseful retreat. A worry began to gather like a thunderstorm in me. I retreated to the feeling of being lost in a gully. All José wanted to know is when we were leaving for the airport. Morning had just broken, and we were leaving at 11:00 a.m. I wanted to scream "Talk to me!" but I couldn't. It was a long, silent, and tense four hours. Silence was often the way José reacted when he was upset or needed time to mull things over. His silence was difficult to endure. I could never feel confident when I feared losing him. God, I wish I hadn't told him.

NIKE's eventual rejection tore my dreams apart. They would not serve as my knights in shining armor. There would be no introductions. Mike Ovitz would never read my book proposal.

José stopped calling.

Finally, all the layers had come off. It was time to do or die. I couldn't let the dream go. It was time to get a computer. It was time to feel the calm that exists at 5:00 a.m. It was time to poke around the memories that so dearly wanted to see their name in print. I was becoming a writer.

****

Penned Moments Revisited

Your silence has resounded in my head before.

Loud, thundering, crackling echoes of nothing.

Nothing said. Nothing to be said.

Good times went on between us, but,

our tomorrows fall on different days.

INDEX

ABOUT THE AUTHOR

Colleen Riley Roberts is an entrepreneur who is now embarking on a career in writing. Throughout her life she wrote hundreds of biographies for the clients she had in the public relations business. Her book, The Life and Times of a Single Woman is about many of the exciting events that formed part of her interesting life. Owning her own press agency, she worked mostly in the world of celebrity. Colleen has also been writing poetry and has incorporated a few of her poems in her memoir. Only beginning to explore avenues for her poetry, any submissions she has made to anthologies have earned her several awards. A British publisher wrote and requested one of her poems which he place on page one of his anthology. This recognition encouraged the writing of her memoir.

Printed in the United States
27225LVS00002B/106-159

9 781418 493844